AF540505

# Economic Participation of Women in Mizoram

## About the Author

**Dr. Lalhriatpuii** is an Assistant Professor in the Department of Economics, Mizoram University. She is the first Mizo woman to be awarded a Ph.D. in Economics. She has participated in a number of workshops/conferences. She has written many seminar papers and research reports on gender inequality, family welfare and on the nature and extent of women's work participation in India.

# ECONOMIC PARTICIPATION OF WOMEN IN MIZORAM

**Lalhriatpuii**

**CONCEPT PUBLISHING COMPANY PVT. LTD.**
**NEW DELHI-110059**

**ISBN:13-978-81-8069-665-7,**

First Published 2010

*Published and Printed by*

**Concept Publishing Company Pvt. Ltd.**
**Regd. Office:**
A/15-16, Commercial Block, Mohan Garden
New Delhi-110059 (India)
*Phones* : 25351460, 25351794, *Fax* : 091-11-25357109
*Email* : publishing@conceptpub.com
*Website:* www.conceptpub.com

**Editorial Office:**
H-13, Bali Nagar, New Delhi-110 015 (India)

Cataloging in Publication Data-- *Courtesy:* D.K. Agencies (P) Ltd. <docinfo@dkagencies.com>

**Lalhriatpuii.**
Economic participation of women in Mizoram / Lalhriatpuii.
p. cm.
Includes bibliographical references (p. ).
Includes index.
ISBN 13: 9788180696657 ISBN 10: 8180696650

1. Women--Employment--India--Mizoram. 2. Women in economic development--India--Mizoram. I. Title.

DDC 331.40954166 22

B. SANGKHUMI
CHAIRPERSON

MIZORAM PUBLIC SERVICE COMMISSION
New Capital Complex, Khatla,
Aizawl, Mizoram-796001 (INDIA)
Off. : 91-389-2335810
Res. : 91-389-2340996, 2343884
Mobile : 09436140298
E-mail : sangkhumi@yahoo.com

# FOREWORD

I feel a great privilege to write a Foreword of a book on 'Economic Participation of Women in Mizoram' by Dr. Lalhriatpuii. It is an immense pleasure to know that Dr. Lalhriatpuii has overcome various obstacles and hurdles to bring out this valuable book. I feel rather proud to know a family like the family of Dr. Lalhriatpuii which respects and supportive to the mother's works even sacrificing the warmth and motherly care on many occasions which every husband and children are expecting from the mother.

It is a matter of great concern and consideration that women, almost 50 per cent of the population, are deprived and discouraged politically, socially and economically even today.

Women Empowerment is a recent notion and effort. Women are active both inside and outside the house but they are still considered inactive and many of them economically unproductive because the women's role in the house is not recognized as productive in economic terms.

Sex discrimination, unemployment, poverty and economic disparities are the main social and economic ailments of a country. Women are the worst sufferers of these melodies, which need remedy.

This book concentrates on problems and prospects of women workers in various economic activities in Mizoram. It also takes into consideration opportunities for women and challenges before women. The status of women in Mizoram both in the rural and urban areas has been empirically viewed under the prevailing demographic, health, economical, educational, social and political situations which will provide an insight to planners, policy makers and researchers.

The author deserves applause and appreciation for bringing out this book on such important issue of economic participation of women in Mizoram. Throughout her research she retained respect for the social life at hand and watchful anxiety about whether she was seeing accurately, which is the difference between an accomplished observer and intellectual imperialist. Like an expert field ecologist, Lalhriatpuii excels at noticing the general in the particular, the particular in the general.

The investigation and findings of the author opens up important new questions while it answers old ones. I hope the book will be useful to students, academicians, social workers, policy makers and policy-takers.

**Mrs. B. Sangkhumi**
Chairperson
Mizoram Public Service Commission
Aizawl, Mizoram

# PREFACE

The condition of poor women has been a major preoccupation of both researchers and activists in India. Looking at this condition, one fact that stands out is the work burden of poor women. The hours of labour that they contribute hardly gets any support either in terms of social inputs like health, education, civic amenities or reduction of the burden of household work, or support in terms of economic inputs like credit, access to raw materials. Yet she persists in providing this labour because of an overriding sense of responsibility for the survival sometimes of her family, sometimes of her new family or perhaps even of society.

Thus, a review of literature in this field, however inadequate, would provide the important missing link to those who are concerned about some of the problems of women Indian society.

So far women have been considered as a group or working force merely to carry on welfare programmes extending to health, education menial and services. But they have more to contribute in the promotion of economic activities and it is evident from the economic role that women play in society in reality.

This book highlights the economic status of women in Mizoram and also identified the structure and determinants of their work participation.

I am thankful to all those unseen hands who have contributed in any way towards bringing up of this book, which I hope will be useful for the social, economic and educated strata of the society who wish to look into women work participation and its various aspects.

**Lalhriatpuii**

# ACKNOWLEDGEMENTS

It is a great pleasure for me to have completed my work entitled *Economic Participation of Women in Mizoram* after overcoming various obstacles and hurdles. I hope that the findings of the study will have important policy implications in the improvement of the status of women in Mizoram.

At the outset, I take this opportunity to express my sincere thanks to Prof. Tlanglawma, for his scholarly guidance, constructive criticisms and the encouragement that had been extended to me throughout the period of my study. I am very fortunate to work under his guidance.

The work would not have been possible without the cooperation of the respondents in the State, I am very grateful to them for candidly sharing their position and ideology which enable me to draw certain conclusions.

I express my deep and everlasting sense of gratitude to my father Sangkhara and my mother Lalhliri, whose unparalleled sacrifice and inspiration throughout my academic career will for ever be a guiding light in my life.

I am also grateful to all the staff of various educational institutions and libraries, for providing easy access to their literature from which indispensable secondary information for the thesis was generated. I express my appreciation to the authorities of Directorate of Economics and Statistics, Mizoram; Directorate of Census Operations, Mizoram, ICSSR and NEHU, Shillong; JNU, Delhi; and State Library of Mizoram, for providing me access to their valuable information.

Throughout the work, my husband K.C. Lalthanthuama and our children K.C. Lalhruaitluanga and K.C. Lalrinhlua, were always supportive, shared my anxieties and concerns. When my role as a mother and wife has to be overshadowed by the present task in hand yet they patiently supported me all along. Words are not enough to express my gratitude for their sacrifice and inspirations.

Above all, I deeply thank Almighty God who has showered me with blessings, mental faculty and sound health.

**Lalhriatpuii**

# CONTENTS

# 1

# INTRODUCTION

## INTRODUCTION

A country can achieve a high rate of economic development through the best and the fullest use of its resources. In a developing country like India, burdened with a huge population, an ideal strategy would be to utilize its human resources to the maximum for a rapid economic growth of the nation. This would necessitate optimum participation of women in the various sectors of economic activity. In the world of today and tomorrow any discrimination between the two sexes in the various occupational fields has no chance to survive, and the sooner females are provided with opportunities to share the task of national development along with the males the better. The central idea is to introduce a work culture among all the able-bodied persons irrespective of their sexes.

India has adopted a policy of planned economic development covering all the segments of growth and sections of society. Naturally women will have to be associated with the process. In India, however, participation of women in economic activities continues to be low. Although new avenues are emerging day by day for female employment, yet they are confined mostly to the tertiary sector, and not providing adequate opportunities for their employment on a larger scale.[1]

Women are understood to have been given a form and image through the imagination of men.[2] A comparison with the nature of work of both the sexes reveals that women have not been able to catch up with men in terms of employment, share of wages, time devoted to work. We use the terms 'catch up' so as to emphasize the point that, in spite of their efficiency, productivity, capability, women have been denied equal footing with men in terms of equal pay, remuneration, decision-making authority and status. Exclusion of women from these rights only retard the progress and development of nation because it is, by now, universally accepted that women workers constitute a meaningful category and their participation along with men constitute the total labour force in the economy.[3]

The development of an economy can be measured not only in terms of GDP, per capita income and wage but also in terms of effective participation and utilization of the capabilities of both men and women as an effective human resource potential.[4] In this context, the economic role of women cannot be isolated from the total framework of development. Equal participation of women is a pre-condition for the development of not only the women but also the country as a whole.

## SIGNIFICANCE OF WOMEN'S WORK PARTICIPATION RATE (WPR)

The entire economic function and activity is related to the process of production, consumption, distribution and exchanges. The individual performs the dual role of a producer and consumer, which is again manifested in his additional role of distributing and exchanging what he produces so as to generate income and to sustain economic activity.[5] But both the activities of being a producer and a consumer are intimately related. For example, the necessity to consume more and thereby to improve the standard of living increases the volume of goods and services, which are produced in the economy. This again is dependent on the quantity and quality of the labour force participating in economically productive occupation. While the former is indicated by the number of persons who are economically active, that is the number of person in the labour force, the latter is reflected in the quality and quantity of skills, productive abilities, motivation and efficiency to work, knowledge acquired and desire to work of the labour force.[6]

While considering the first aspect of participation, the relative participation in economic activities have been different among the sexes and also have been showing different trends of activities varying from one region to another and from time to time. Women's subsequent role in the patriarchal set-up enshrined in India took the final form around the third century.[7]

Depending on the needs and requirements of the household a woman needs to oscillate between wide varieties of tasks whether productive or unproductive. The ideologies such as chastity and frequent motherhood prevent women from entering the labour market and in situations where they do; it is by compulsive economic condition like poverty and deprivation. While the economic necessity and the need for supplementing family income could be the major factors for women to enter the labour market, economic transformation could also be cited to constitute an equally important reason.[8] Therefore, study of Female Work Participation Rate (FWPR) is needed in the context of improving the status of women which does not necessarily increase only with an increase in the participation rate but along with an increase in the ability to claim wages and to take an active part in the decision-making process.

## WOMEN WORK PARTICIPATION IN INDIA

Involved in an unbelievable variety and multiplicity of activities millions of Indian women live and work below poverty line, their sole purpose being to provide for the survival need of their families. Their multiple roles as workers, child bearers and rearers and family maintenance through a variety of overlapping activities account for the much debated invisibility and undervaluation of their labour.

Women constitute a significant part of the workforce in India. But the WPR continues to be substantially less for females than for males. Majority of women workers are employed in the rural areas. Of the total rural women workers, 87 per cent of them are employed in agriculture as labourers and cultivators. Amongst women workers in urban areas, about 80 per cent are employed in the unorganised sector like household industries, petty commercial trade and services etc. The ILO highlighted that female work participation rate varies from one place to another due to different economic, social and cultural conditions prevailing in each region. Therefore, the social condition, in general, has come in the way of participation of women in the economic activities in India.[9]

It is by now unanimously accepted that women play an important role in the economic development of a nation. The development of an economy can be measured not only in terms of GDP, per capita income and wage but it needs to be seen also in terms of effective participation and utilization of the capabilities of both men and women as an effective human resource potential. In this context, the economic role of women cannot be isolated from the total framework of development. Equal participation is a pre-condition for the development of not only the women but also the country as a whole. Emancipation of women and their equality with men are impossible as long as women are excluded from economic productive work and confined to work involving only child bearing, rearing and supervision of the household. The existence of the concept of inequality of the sexes requires that in the present context we rescue the notion of gender from its ritualistic incantations and make it effectively work for a more emancipatory and inclusive social order.[10]

The force of tradition had been overcome by factors like literacy and educational levels of women in countries where female workforce participation rate is high in the labour market. However, the common feature is that women as weaker section and on gender consideration suffer from market discrimination and are hence pushed to low status of jobs. However, labour force participation has shown a rising trend.[11] This is possible due to economic structure.

## DISCRIMINATION

It may be observed that certain issues/changes have occurred in women labour market in the last three decades. Tradition alone does not prevent a change of sex roles in the labour market and there are other factors also. It is "employer's interest" which brings a sharp demarcation between male and female jobs. In many cases employers reserve jobs for women as it would be done more cheaply. In some countries, women are paid less than men for equal work. In yet another country, unequal pay can be maintained by classifying certain jobs for women and placing these jobs in a lower category than male job that require same level of qualification.[12]

Productivity of a woman to generate income is closely related to the amount of space allocated to her to operate independently as an economic agent. In majority of cases though it is observed that allocation of space is very much restricted as women are considered to be flexible resource in the work participation process. This hypothesis is based on the ground reality that in majority of the households, investment in women in the form of training, education for any particular skill or field of operation is considered to be either wasteful or ignored. As a result women are treated as a flexible resource adaptably reserved for any numerous jobs that are allocated to them. This, perhaps, could be one of the reasons why women labour supply is more intimately connected to their own family income levels than to wage rate in their jobs. This widespread discrimination has led feminist concern to claim for equal pay for men and women workers. But this demand, as some researchers believe, increases the cost of employing women workers and, therefore, male workers are replacing them. The existence of discriminated wages with regard to women is explained on the ground that women have less vocational training and less employment unlike man for the same occupation.[13]

Visaria[14] pointed out that for all manual operations, men are paid higher wages than women. Most of the occupations are held in the public or the organised private sector, with more or less fixed salary scales. In other occupations female workers suffer clear disadvantages in earnings.

Discrimination against women continues in employment as women get lower wages in spite of the law to enforce equal pay for equal work and fewer women are in top jobs. Thousands of women are involved in the small-scale sector or in home based industries. But their supervisors or contractors are all men. As a result women are severally exploited both on wages and conditions of work.[15]

Apart from wage discrimination, which exists in the labour market, there also exists a wide gap between what women contribute to the economy and the remuneration they receive even when women perform the same work as men.

## DISCRIMINATION IN INDIA

In India, discrimination in the labour force exists in various forms: discriminatory wages, occupational segregation, human capital discrimination and so on. In spite of these discriminatory structures, which operate in the labour market, women's entry in the paid labour force has increased significantly over the years due to rapid industrialization, structural reforms and an increased desire to better off the standard of living.[16] But the increase in female labour force participation has not led to women achieving equal status or bargaining power in the labour market as claimed for. Increase in wages is increasingly being associated with a simultaneous increase in productivity. For example, women's concentration in the services sector has contributed to an overall weakening of their wage bargaining power since increased productivity is not easily measured in this sector. A major barrier to equality for women in the market place is also the discrimination in hiring, promotion and wages.[17]

In unorganised sectors as well as in rural areas women are paid much less than men for the same job. In case of construction work contractors cheat them out of their legitimate wages. In agriculture the concentration of working women is more and we also find wage discrimination in this sector in spite of the Minimum Wages and Payment of Wages Act. In occupation like garment making domestic service which does not come under the purview of the minimum wages legislation, the condition is still worse. Barring a small section of highly educated women in the selected profession and careers most of the working women are paid much less than men doing the same job. The enforcement machinery also operates with various constraints as a result of which this problem is becoming serious.[18]

Besides general problems working women also face some occupation specific problems. Mention may be made here that in *beedi* making and tobacco processing women workers are paid much less than the prescribed minimum wages. Many a time they are not issued identity cards to prove their permanent nature of jobs. As a result they are not entitled to social security benefits and welfare measures.[19]

Wage or pay discrimination also referred to as direct discrimination is a common feature of the Indian labour market, where wage differential exists between two equally efficient male and female not on the basis of productivity differences but on the basis of sex. Prevalence of sex segregation has been the principal explanatory factor explaining this behaviour.

Occupational segregation takes two forms, viz. horizontal segregation and vertical segregation. Several studies have identified a positive correlation between the level of occupational segregation size of modern activities and diversification of activities.[20] In spite of women's rapid advancement in terms of education and skill, occupational segregation has not really decreased and from the economic point of view, it is certainly considered as inefficiency or market failure since the potentialities and capabilities of female human capital are not being optimally allocated according to their productive potential.[21] The economic results of occupational segregation for women are low wages and are relegated to positions where productivity and experience have little implications on their status as they advance in age.

An essential prerequisite for woman in the labour market is her being flexible resource adaptable to various changes. She is definitely considered as an economic agent and a participant in economic activity. Yet woman never trained nor being made specialized or aware of a particular skill or job but is always seen as a supplementary factor of production. Her work, therefore, is always considered peripheral. According to Kalpagam[22] this assumption about the malleability and flexibility of labour is particularly detrimental to women's work. She also explains that wage discrimination is due to the fact that there is a common accepted notion that men are more efficient than women and women's income is only a supplementary earning while men are considered as principal earners.

## DEFICIENCIES IN PROMOTIONAL MEASURES TO MINIMIZE DISCRIMINATION

In recent years with an emphasis to empower women, various activities have been promoted to generate self-employment among women. But even with regard to self-employed incomes, it becomes difficult to distinguish the women component of most of these activities, as most of it falls under household activity, which does not enter the market. The same is not specific for men because a majority of their products is marketed and calculated.[23] Though the share of self-employed workers has increased in recent years, men have been capable of investing and venturing into own business while women who constitute a sizeable proportion of the workers are usually engaged as co-workers and have no independent control over matters related to decision-making.[24]

Through the help of various social activists and NGOs, working conditions in various informal sectors have been formalized. But when it comes to the task of assessing the work of women it is observed that a large proportion of women's work is concentrated in jobs involving minimum scope for improvement with low pay and status as compared to men.[25]

An interesting trend that has affected the mental attitude of many rising unemployed men in recent years is that 'too much emancipation of women' have brought along with it social problems, family discord and growing unemployment among men. A growing number of men feel that much of these social tensions could be eased if women resort to their traditional roles as good mothers and good wives. In this context feminists argue that patriarchal measures, such as extended maternity leave and early retirement have been introduced to encourage women to stay at home. As a result, there is little sensitivity to women's issues and to growing "Feminisation of unemployment".[26]

Numerous studies highlight the fact that structural reforms and liberalization policies are often distributed disproportionately, so that women are forced to bear a greater share of the burden. Although trade liberalization in the developing countries has led to a steep increase in the participation of women in the export oriented industries, providing them with new opportunities and challenges but the quality of most of these jobs are poor and insecure. Women are paid only a fraction of male wage for the same nature of work and lacked social protection. It cannot, therefore, be denied that there exists simultaneously a strong positive relationship between economic growth and economic advancement of women.

Overall it may be summarized that, though the participation of women has been increasing in recent years, women have a lower employment status than men. Majority of women concentrate in lower category of jobs and this phenomenon is present both in the organised and unorganised sector of the labour market.[27] While men are found to be employed in primary market jobs, which are characterized by qualified jobs, providing high wages, better working conditions, job security and internal job ladder,[28] in contrast women are employed in secondary job market, which tends to have low benefits and wages, high labour turn over and less job mobility. As a result, women are poorly represented. Casual workers are predominantly women and are hired or paid on a daily wage basis and are not covered by any contract or labour laws.[29]

Similarly the unemployment rates among women are consistently higher than men irrespective of how unemployment was defined. It is also evident in NSSO studies between 1983 and 1993, that women unemployment has been found to be higher both in the urban and rural India as compared to men. This also explains the low share of women in labour market and consequently lowers employment status than men.[30]

SOCIO-ECONOMIC PROFILE OF MIZORAM

## Location, Area and Topography

Mizoram is a small State lying approximately between 21°.58′N to 24°.35′N latitude and 92°.15′E to 93°.29′E longitude. The total geographical area of the State is 21,087 sq.km., constituting about 0.64 per cent of the total area of India.[31] It has a strategic location having international boundaries with Myanmar in the east and south, Bangladesh and of Tripura in the west. Further, the Cachar district of Assam and Manipur bound the State in the north. Mizoram has about 404 km. length of international boundary with Myanmar and 316 km. length with Bangladesh.

The topography of Mizoram consists predominantly of mountainous terrain of tertiary rocks. The mountain ranges run north to south direction in parallel series. These ranges are separated from one another by narrow and deep river valley with only a few and small patches of flat lands lying in between them. The terrain of Mizoram is young and so the geomorphic features do not show much diversity in the formation of the landforms. Most of the landforms observed are of erosion nature.

The drainage system of the State consists of a number of small rivers and streams. Most of them are of ephemeral nature, depending on monsoon rains. Their volume and level fluctuate greatly in dry and rainy seasons. Most of the drainage lines originated in the central part of the State and flow towards either north or south influenced by the north-south trending ridges. The main rivers of the State are Tlawng, Tuirial, Tuivawl, all flowing northwards and Tiau, Chimtuipui, Khawthlangtuipui all flowing southwards.

## Climate and Rainfall

Mizoram being located on a tropical region enjoys a moderate climate. It falls under the direct influence of the

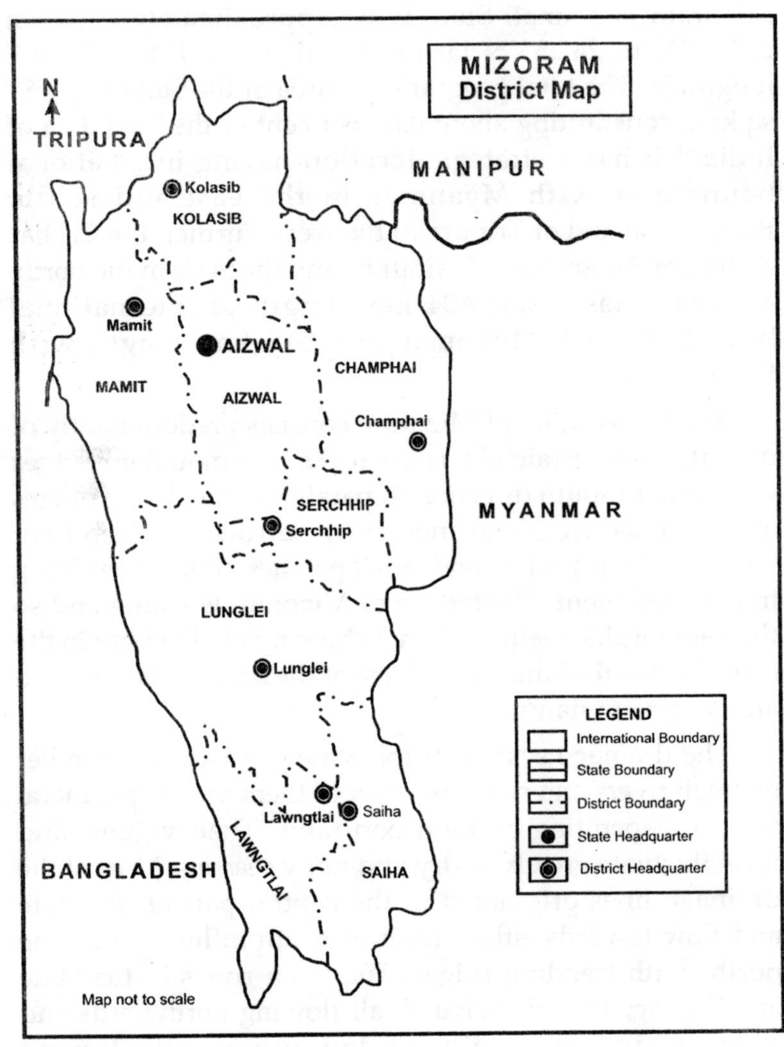


*Source* : www.mapsofIndia.com

south-west monsoon and as such, the region receives adequate rainfall. The climate is humid and tropical featured by short winter and long summer with heavy rainfall. The summer temperature ranges from 25°C to 29°C, whereas it is 18°C to 25°C in autumn and 11°C to 23°C in winter.

The average rainfall in Mizoram is about 250 cm per year, though it may increase to 350 cm in the north-west part of the State. Generally, it rains during May to September; July and August being the rainiest months. November to January are dry months with minimum rainfall.

**Table 1.1:** Monthly Average Rainfall in Mizoram
(For the last 5 years)

*(in mm)*

| Month | 2001 | 2002 | 2003 | 2004 | 2005 |
|---|---|---|---|---|---|
| January | 0 | 21 | 1 | - | 3 |
| February | 44 | 1 | 8 | - | 11 |
| March | 45 | 70 | 82 | 14 | 150 |
| April | 91 | 142 | 139 | 350 | 111 |
| May | 393 | 567 | 282 | 260 | 300 |
| June | 531 | 368 | 740 | 568 | 186 |
| July | 369 | 556 | 313 | 669 | 409 |
| August | 341 | 443 | 367 | 383 | 355 |
| September | 326 | 259 | 377 | 371 | 321 |
| October | 295 | 135 | 196 | 131 | 213 |
| November | 99 | 85 | - | 4 | 25 |
| December | 1 | 1 | 42 | - | 9 |
| Annual Average | 2535 | 2648 | 2546 | 2751 | 2094 |

*Source: Statistical Handbook of Mizoram, 2006.*

## Social and Cultural Background

The original homeland of the Mizo people is believed to be somewhere in China. However, in the absence of any written records and other evidences, the early historical account of Mizo society simply rely on oral tradition in the form of folktales and folksongs. Since there is no concrete evidence about the origin of the Mizo people, there are divergent views in respect of the original homeland of the Mizos and their migratory route from their early habitat to their present settlement in India, Myanmar and Bangladesh.

It is believed that the Mizos had confined their settlement in the Kabaw valley especially around Khampat in Myanmar from the middle of ninth century to late thirteenth century A.D. They left the area due to the attacks made by the powerful Shan tribe. Later, they moved to the present Chin Hills and some of them went as far as their present settlement in the various parts of North East Region of India. The Mizo people have a rich and varied colourful cultural heritage, which are preserved and enriched till today. The majority of the Mizo are Christians. The 88.49 percentage of literacy in 2001 Census is indebted to the British Christian missionaries. Earlier, the Mizos used to observe three kinds of festivals or *Kut*. *Pawl Kut* is held at the end of a harvest. It falls some time between December and January. *Mim Kut* is another festival observed in remembrance of the dead. It is held in August and September. The most popular and enjoyable one is *Chapchar Kut*, which is observed during March and April.

In the early socio-political system, the Chief ruled the village with the support of the village elders. The chief had supreme authority over the affairs of the villages. Each village had their own bachelors' dormitory called *Zawlbuk* which was at the heart and centre of the village life and provided security and defence for the whole village.

The British annexed Mizoram in 1890. The Mizos came under the influence of western Christian missionaries in the later part of the ninteenth century and now a majority of them practice Christianity with devotion. The Mizo society is a close-knit one and it attaches great importance to kinship, social relations and co-operation.

THE STATUS OF WOMEN IN MIZORAM

## Background

Although the condition of women in Mizoram is comparatively better than in other States of the country, yet, the position in the traditional Mizo society was not much different from that of the position given to women elsewhere in the country.

The traditional Mizo society is based strictly on what is known as extreme patriarchal society of institution in which women are reduced practically to second-class citizen or slave. Within the narrow sense of the marriage contract as per the customary law, woman can be bought or sold by fixing a nominal bride's price amounting to just about Rs. 400 to Rs. 500 only. Besides if a man has a child with a girl outside the wedlock, he has to pay a pittance of the bastard's price of Rs. 40 only.

Women do not have practically any saying in all the decision-making whether at home or outside. They are supposed to contribute in the process of procreation and it is their duty to rear and nurture the children in addition to the daily household or domestic' works. They are not supposed to have any independent religious loyalty, but they are required to follow the religion of their husbands. Discrimination against women is still prevalent even in church and other social organizations. Women are, till today, not eligible to become church elder or pastor of the church. They never occupy the top position in any social institutions or NGOs.[32]

One of the most important discrimination against women in Mizo society is the right of inheritance. Strictly according to the customary law, women are not entitled to any inheritance to family or ancestral property. If there is no son in the family, the family property including the ancestral home should go to the nephew of the father, as the daughters including the mother of the family cannot keep the family property after the death of the family father. This is an extreme case of deprivation for women.

### *Education*

Before the coming of the Missionaries into their land Mizos did not have written language/written scripts. All were in oral form. It was J.H. Lorraine and F.W. Savidge, the Missionaries who came to Mizoram and took it upon themselves to develop the Mizo language into writing, introducing the Roman script. The Missionaries adopted education as the most important means of spreading Christianity and within a short period of 50 years a significant percentage of the population of Mizoram became educated.

Mizoram was a late starter in the field of education. Only in 1948 Mizoram could produce High School Leaving Certificate (HSLC) candidates. In that year, in all there were 23 candidates (Mizo), out of which 11 were females. This is amazing considering that women have to struggle hard for continuing their education. Importance of literacy should never be ignored. Its contribution to the life and well-being of the people deserved our attention. Literacy rate of Mizoram is second highest in the country next only to Kerala. Table 1.2 shows the literacy rate of Mizoram and India over the past three decades.

**Table 1.2:** Literacy Rate

*(in percentage)*

| Year | MIZORAM | | | INDIA | | |
|---|---|---|---|---|---|---|
| | Total | Males | Females | Total | Males | Females |
| 1971 | 53.79 | 60.49 | 46.71 | 34.45 | 45.95 | 21.97 |
| 1981 | 59.88 | 64.46 | 54.91 | 43.56 | 56.37 | 29.75 |
| 1991 | 82.27 | 85.65 | 78.60 | 52.11 | 63.86 | 39.42 |
| 2001 | 88.49 | 90.69 | 86.13 | 65.38 | 75.85 | 54.16 |

*Source:* Census of India Reports, 1971-2001.

Mizoram has done quite well in literacy percentage as compared to her neighbouring states. Table 1.2 shows that in 2001 out of the total literacy (88.49 per cent) of the State, male literacy is 90.69 per cent and female literacy is 86.13 per cent. The national literacy is 65.38 per cent, of which male literacy is 75.85 per cent and female literacy is 54.16

per cent. Mizoram has done quite well in the field of literacy in general and women literacy in particular. This has a far-reaching effect in the position and status of women in the society.

***Work Participation***

Until recently economic role of women did not attract much attention in Mizoram because much of women's work is done at home or outside the formal economy. It is now clear that the economic role of women cannot be isolated from the process of development, so the need is to better understand the issue. Women constitute a significant part of the workforce in Mizoram. But their participation in the process of economic development is not given due importance. Employment of women is a matter of vital importance for their economic empowerment. Table 1.3 shows the distribution of workers in Mizoram.

One of the interesting aspects of female participation in the work sphere in Mizoram is the concentration of female workers in the primary sector, as cultivators and agricultural labourers. Not only that the percentage of their participation is quite high but also it has shown an increasing trend especially as agricultural labourers. This compels one to think that lack of employment opportunities forces the female workers to concentrate in the agricultural and allied activities.

Work place discrimination occurs between men and women who have equal productivity and tastes for working conditions, but with unequal wages, treatment and access to jobs. Employment and earning patterns lay out a consistent picture of women predominantly occupying low-paid jobs and working less than men. These patterns are viewed as evidence of discrimination.

Women also supply a major portion of labour in the production of cash crops. But there is discrimination against women. While women are usually responsible for the strenuous job of weeding and transplanting, men control the production of commercial crops and derive profits by selling such crops. With an increase in the density of population land becomes divided, sub-divided and fragmented. So women are required to walk longer and longer distances, as they have to move from one field to another.

Due to resource constraints and risk of financial investments women in female-headed households are forced to remain engaged in traditional modes of economic activity. As a result their productivity stagnates while that of men continues to rise. Since they are generally restricted to low-productivity informal sector employment and have to bear higher dependency burdens, they invariably remain poor and malnourished and do not stand a strong chance to obtain formal education, healthcare, or sanitation. In fact, the economic welfare of women and children within poor families depend to a considerable extent on the economic status of women. This means that just as per capita income is an inadequate measure of absolute poverty; household income is also a poor measure of individual welfare. The reason is that distribution of income within the household may be quite unequal.

Many women run small family businesses, called micro enterprises, which require very little initial capital and often involve the marketing of food articles and handicrafts produced under the domestic system. No doubt women's limited access to capital leads to higher rates of return on their tiny investments. But the unbelievably low capital-labour ratios confine women to low productivity undertakings.

It is obvious that in successive census, the concept of worker has been changing and some do not get a comparable data of women and their exact contribution to economic work. There is an exclusion of a whole range of activities performed by women. The unpaid economic activities; their contribution in work through domestic sectors, their long hours of household work remain unaccounted. The productivity of women in Mizoram is high as compared to the average Indian women. Vegetable markets, petty shops etc. are run by them. They have an immeasurable contribution in the sustenance of family, shaping the destiny of the people and of the society. All these issues need proper investigation. The contributions of women must be accounted for and treated as essential factors in the economic growth of the country.

***Decision-making in the Society***

In a deeply communitarian society like Mizoram where social life is free, and men and women mixed together freely, it is not possible to make rigid distinction between male and female in work areas. It is, therefore, possible for an outside observer to think that in Mizoram there is no distinction between men and women as stated by Dutta[33] when he states that the interdependence and the mutual appreciation of each other's position and responsibilities "appears to point out that the status of women in their society was in no way inferior to that of men and hence suffered none of these derogatory and discriminatory treatment as may be found in some of the more advanced societies". This judgment may not be entirely accurate in the sense that when compared with the social life of traditional Hindus and Muslims, Mizo society is indeed free so far as the mixing up of men and women are concerned. But the fact remains that in spite of all their social freedom and their significant contributions in the family, Mizo women are not liberated and they are regarded as subordinate to men and they are very much discriminated against in various aspects of life. Many examples may be pointed out concerning women whose earning is controlled by their husbands and ill treated by them in spite of their earning and women who do household work but are subsequently divorced by their husbands.

Women are excluded in all decision-making bodies in both social organisations and church life. While the condition of women has considerably improved in government sectors, there is no corresponding improvement so far as their status and placement in church is concerned. Ever since the coming of Christianity and establishment of the church in Mizoram women played an important role in evangelisation work and in various aspects of life. They continue to be the limbs of the church in various ways. Women continue to play assisting roles only and even trained women do not get their right job and responsibilities in the church. They are excluded from various decision-making bodies, ordination and other responsible positions. Church plays a dominant role in Mizo society. Therefore, the criterion of judgment of a developing church or State is the condition of women, the way they are treated and regarded and the type of jobs they are given.

Since women are a group of people who are oppressed most, they need empowerment, which will release them from oppression. We speak of the need of development of our church and State. If we really want to develop them, we must first think of developing women, for no real development can come without women's development. I.K. Gujral in a message delivered on the 50th Independence Day rightly stress that without the development of women no country can attain real development.

### *Local Administration*

Villages are governed by Village Council wherein women seldom have a chance to gain membership. Women need to be empowered to take part in the level of village/town administration. In the Village Council election of 2002 out of 532 Village Councils, only 48 women were elected as members and only 2 out of them are selected as council president. In the recent election of February 2006, only 36 women were selected as members from the 556 villages and out of which 3 are elected as president. Therefore, it is urgent to find ways and means to include more women in decision-making as a source of empowerment.

### *Political Field*

In political field women participate as voters but their participation is nil as leadership. The only way women participate actively in politics is by supporting their husbands or relatives at the time of their election campaign. Even when women decide to contest election at the Assembly level their chance of winning is quite low as traditional Mizo society still look at men as their leaders and when some women attempt to climb the ladder, the notion that women are not worthy to be a leader is still very strong which in turn, strongly govern people's mindset. From the record of the election history of Mizoram only one Mizo lady has so far been elevated to the position of Minister of State in the Legislative Assembly.

It is imperative that women need empowerment and strong support in different social organisations, village/town/municipal level administration and politics. Verbal encouragement will be of very little help. They have to be trained to take up responsibilities and opportunities, and then only empowerment will work. At the same time, on the part of women too it is necessary to accept responsibilities and learn to develop self-esteem, to claim that they are able and can do it.

In spite of various forms of activities, women of Mizoram are yet to see the face of the true form of women emancipation and development. The economy suffers from various infrastructural and development deficiencies. Unemployment is rampant in the areas with no simultaneous development or growth of job-generating sectors. Though this concern both men and women alike, but the problems faced by women are more acute. Therefore, striving towards equality between the sexes is a much 'market compatible approach' and also in consonance with prevalent macro economic policies.[34] Thus, women need to be viewed and empowered on an equal footing with men in all spheres of life.

## NECESSITY OF THE WORK AND IMPACT OF FEMALE WORK PARTICIPATION RATE (FWPR) IN MIZO SOCIETY

To identify the need for studying FWPR (Female Work Participation Rate), we look at the WPR among Women in East and South East Asia, where there is a high work participation rate. This is probably due to relatively less social restrictions and taboos associated with women working outside and also due to high literacy rate in those countries demanding a greater role amongst women in the participatory process.[35] Bangladesh and Pakistan mark a comparatively low figure than India. Though considerable work has been done to examine the casual factors behind such low participation, India's position is still far behind the trend that is observed in other Asian countries and fall short of the progress achieved by some of the industrialized countries with respect to WPR.

Conceptual variation on measurement factors have been cited as the main reason behind the low FWPR but disparity in FWPR is a universal phenomenon differing only in intensity and magnitude from one country to another. In advanced countries, FWPR is on the increase,[36] which indicates that women are gradually being aware of their role and need for effective participation. But for countries like India, this awareness is yet to show its presence. Therefore, FWPR needs to be studied to examine the low FWPR with respect to other developed and industrialized economies and also to examine the factors such as cultural and economic perception which control to a large extent the participation rate of female in India.

We now analyse the FWPR with respect to the overall situation of India and Mizoram. Table 1.3 shows the WPR during the period 1971 to 2001.

**Table 1.3:** Work Participation Rates of Males and Females

| Years | INDIA | | MIZORAM | |
|---|---|---|---|---|
| | Male | Female | Male | Female |
| 1971 | 52.50 | 19.69 | – | – |
| 1981 | 51.09 | 19.08 | 56.04 | 43.06 |
| 1991 | 51.08 | 22.05 | 55.18 | 44.82 |
| 2001 | 68.40 | 31.59 | 56.29 | 43.70 |

*Source:* Census of India Reports, 1971–2001.

Table 1.3 presents a disorderly visual impression of participation rates over the different census periods, in which the concept of workers was revised at every census enumeration.[37] The above figure indicates a decreasing participation of males during 1971 to 1991 and a slightly increasing participation for females at the national level. However, 2001 census shows sudden increase in the participation for both the sexes. It may be noted here that female participation is much lower than the male both at Mizoram and the country as a whole. The gap between male and female participation rate was much wider at the national level than in Mizoram. Women's participation in economic activity has been increasing over the years with a far-reaching implication not only in the quality of human resources but also in terms of the level of participation of a working population.[38] This has been possible due to various factors like education and general awareness for empowerment and economic independence for women.

Thus, a study of FWPR assumes utmost importance to understand the implications. It is apparent that with the overall population increasing, FWPR in Mizoram and India as a whole is much lower than MWPR. With the increasing population, combined with poor representation in the total workforce, the unemployment among the female population is found to be alarming.

The change in female labour force participation has not led to a simultaneous increase in women achieving equal status or bargaining power in the labour market, which is closely related, to increase in productivity. The high concentration of women in sectors involving daily household chores, family farm unit and strenuous routine work has contributed to the weakening of their wage bargaining power since increased productivity is not easily measured in this sector. Reports of the Commission on the status of women[39] have shown that women's earnings are lower than man in most of the reporting countries. Thus FWPR also needs to be studied in the context of improving the status of women which does not necessarily increase with an increase in the participation rate.

## CONCLUSION

Since the last few decades the traditional society of India and the status of women have been undergoing a series of changes. Urbanisation, education, migration and other socio-cultural and economic factors are really changing the original arena of Indian society and the female participation in different areas and employment pattern in India. There have been significant changes in the women's work scenario in the last two decades especially during the 1980s in both developed and developing countries. Irrespective of differing rates of work participation there is general agreement that women are subjected to labour market discrimination and are segregated to low paying status and low jobs. The argument is that women are pushed to periphery in terms of their employment and this is sometimes referred to as feminisation of occupations,[40] which contributes to marginalizing the economic role of women in the process of economic development. With the cost of living going up women have started entering otherwise hitherto male dominated field of employment. But this diversification of work opportunities has also brought along with it several adverse consequences for women workers in terms of working and work conditions.

In Mizoram, the situation is nowhere different. Women form a major component of the workforce and are engaged in various forms of agricultural work along with men but major part of their activities remain unrecognized and unremunerated. Lacks of modernization in the rural sector have penalized women as the number of women working in agriculture and related activities are quite high. Though important changes have been taking place in the levels of literacy and the more women are to be found in decision-making and managerial positions. This description of women's employment has not changed over time from a macro perspective. The increased entry of women in the labour market and the changing economic role of women in the household have led to substantial impact on the work structure.

With increased participation of women in the labour force, the economic role of women has improved over the years in India as well as in Mizoram. However, they are concentrated heavily in agriculture, manual and casual work. The scenario of increasing labour market entry of women and a case study in relation to Mizoram would help in better understanding of the micro economic participation of women in various activities and their status thereof in relation to men.

NOTES

1. Delamont, Sara (2003): *Feminist Sociology*, Sage Publication, London.
2. Bagchi, J. (1995): *Indian Women Myth and Reality*, Sangam Books, Hyderabad.
3. Beneria Lordes (1978): *Production, Reproduction and the Sexual Division of Labour*, ILO Working Paper, pp. 14.
4. John E. Mary (1996): Gender and Development in India, 1970s - 1990s : Some Reflections on the Constitutive Role of Contents, *Economic and Political Weekly*.
5. Chaudhary, R.K. (1992): *Work Participation and Economic Status of Women*, Omsons Publishers, New Delhi.
6. Mitra, J. (1997): *Women and Society, Equality and Empowerment*, Kanishka Publishers, New Delhi.

7. Boserup, E. (1970): *Women's Role in Economic Development*, George Allen and Unwin, London.
8. Banerjee, N. (1995): *Labour Institute and the New Economic Order in India*, International Development Studies, Rosskilde University, Denmark.
9. ILO (1987): *World Labour Report*, Oxford University Press.
10. John E. Mary (1996): Gender and Development in India, 1970s – 1990s : Some Reflections on the Constitutive Role of Contents, *Economic and Political Weekly*.
11. Leon, C.B. (1981): The Employment-Population Ratio: Its Value in Labour Force Analysis, *Monthly Labour Review*, Vol. 104, No. 2.
12. Parthasarthy, G. and Dasaradharma Rao (1981): *Women in the Labour Force in India*, ILO-ARTEP.
13. Atmanand (1990): *Women Labour Force: Trend and Pattern of Employment*, Khadi Gramodyog.
14. Visaria, P. (1999): Level and Pattern of Female Employment, in *Gender and Employment in India*, T.S Papola and A.N. Sharma (Ed.), Vikas Publishing House Ltd., New Delhi.
15. Desai, A.S. (1999): Women in Higher Education and National Development, *University News*, Vol. 37, No. 9.
16. Unni, J. (2001): Gender and Informality in Labour Market in South Asia, *Economic and Political Weekly*, No. 26, 30th June.
17. Leftwich H. Richard, Ansel and Sharp M. (1984), *Economics of Social Issues*, Business Publications, Plano, Texas.
18. Sujjaya, C. (1995): Women's Rights and Development Policies in India, *The Administrator*, Vol.XL, July–September.
19. Sharma, A. and Singh, S. (1993): *Women and Work: Changing Scenario in India*, Indian Society of Labour Economics, B.R. Publications, New Delhi.
20. Bakker Isabel (1988): *Women's Employment in Comparative Perspective*, Oxford University Press, New York.
21. Rothbeck, S. and Sarthi, A. (1999): Gender Based Segregation in the Indian Labour Market, *Indian Journal of Labour Economics*, Vol. 42, No. 4.
22. Kalpagam, U. (1997): *Informal Sector: Emerging Perspective in Development*, Seminar Paper, Dec. 22-24, IAMR-IHD, New Delhi.
23. Unni, J. (2001): Gender and Informality in Labour Market in South Asia, *Economic and Political Weekly*, No. 26, 30th June.

24. Banerjee, N. (1999): Women in Emerging Labour Market, *The Indian Journals of Labour Economics*, Vol. 42, No. 4.
25. Eapen, M. (2001): Women in the Informal Sector in Kerala Need for Re-examination, *Economic and Political Weekly*, June 30.
26. Commission on the Status of Women: *Feminisation of Unemployment*, 39th Session, New York, 1995.
27. Rothbeck, S. and Sarthi, A. (1999): Gender Based Segregation in the Indian Labour Market, *Indian Journal of Labour Economics*, Vol. 42, No. 4.
28. Thurow Lester C. (1975): *Poverty and Discrimination*, D.C. Brooklyn Institution, Washington.
29. Acharya and Jose (1991): *Employment and Mobility: A Study among Workers of Low Income Households in Bombay City*, ARTEP Working Paper, ILO, New Delhi.
30. Jose, A.V. (1987): *Limited Options: Women Workers in Rural India*, ILO, ARTEP, New Delhi.
31. *Statistical Handbook of Mizoram, 2006*, Directorate of Economics and Statistics, Govt. of Mizoram.
32. Lalhriatpuii (2006): *Status of Women: Focus Mizoram–Past Trends and Desirable Perspective*, Seminar Paper on Emancipation of Women, NE-ICSSR, Shillong. *(being published)*
33. Dutta Ray, B.B. (1978): *Social and Economic Profile of N.E India*, B.R. Publishing Corporation, Delhi.
34. Verrier, Elwin (1976): *Tribal Women in Indian Women*, edited by Jain, Devaki, Delhi: Publications Division, Ministry of Information and Broadcasting, Govt. of India (reprint).
35. Dreze and Sen (1996): *India Economic Development and Social Security*, Oxford University Press, New York.
36. Gupta, A.K. (1986): *Women and Society: The Development Perspective*, Criterion Publications, Delhi.
37. *See Appendix II.*
38. Iyer, K.V. (1967): The Increasing Role of Women in Economic and Social Development, *Social Welfare*, Vol. 14, No. 7.
39. Commission on the Status of Women (1995) : *Feminisation of Unemployment*, 39th Session, New York.
40. Derek, Robinson (2002): *Differences in Occupational Earnings by Sex*, in Martha Fetherolf Loutfi (ed.), *Women, Gender and Work*, ILO, Geneva.

2

# THEORETICAL BACKGROUND AND CONCEPTUAL FRAMEWORK

## INTRODUCTION

Women's liberation movement as well as feminist economists has from time to time brought into focus a very important point. The statistical evidence of an increase in female employment does not by itself imply a marked strengthening of women's position in the labour market. On the other hand an increasing number of female participation in the labour force both in the developed as well as in the developing economies, have brought into focus the sharp wage differences in the labour market. Apart from monetary gaps that exist between males and females, there also exists discrimination in the form of vertical, horizontal segregation and sex segregation in the job market. While many economic and social scientists feel that gender-based discrimination have been reduced over the years there still exists a significant difference between the earnings of men and women.[1] What is more alarming is that these differences are systematically correlated with other non-economic factors such as social, cultural, regional etc.

The history of female employment in gainful professions outside the family in India is recent one. It is only during recent times that the women of our country are getting exposed to outside world and are trying to learn certain skills to be in employment along with the males. Apart from economic necessities there are other reasons for employment of women, these reasons relate to desire for economic independence, utilization of her individual talent, supplementing the family income, trying to secure equality of status, and utilizing time and energy in order to reduce monotony and boredom from her domestic life.

In this connection several theories have tried to examine the growing necessity of women's participation in labour market and the type of segregation that exists. A study of these theories, therefore, becomes necessary to understand how far these theories have really been able to address the issues of segregation and discrimination that exists or prevails in the labour market with Mizoram as a case study. This is necessary because a deprivation of women in gainful opportunities in employment has an impact on their personal development, quality of life, which ultimately leads to a waste of human resources.

This chapter, therefore, makes an attempt to investigate the theoretical perspective of gender discrimination that exists and to understand the various feminists viewpoint and labour theories on unequal relations in the labour market. This is necessary to reconcile economic growth with equitable distribution of benefits among men and women, equality of power relations and also to understand the interdependence and partnership between them.

## GENDER DISCRIMINATION : A THEORETICAL PERSPECTIVE

Discrimination can be defined as 'unequal treatment in terms and conditions of employment for groups of equally productive workers'.[2] Discrimination can also be defined as recognition and understanding of the difference between one thing and another.

Discrimination arises when we distinguish human resources on the basis of individual efforts and productivity. Discrimination could exist in various forms and magnitudes.

The different forms of discrimination such as employment discrimination, occupational discrimination and price discrimination do affect women in various stages of their entry into labour market, which leads the gap in the female-male earnings. Two basic reasons for this earning gap are: one, the majority of women is in occupation where the chances of advancement are very limited. And two, the significant rise in the female labour force has kept a larger proportion of women at the lower rung of pay.[3]

It is generally accepted that inequality between men and women stems from attitudes, prejudices and assumptions concerning the different role assigned to men and women in society. These roles, which are learned, e.g., those of parents, housekeeper, provider of basic needs, etc. largely determine the type of work men and women do. For example given their traditional role as homemakers, more female than male workers tend to combine economic activities with household (non-economic) activities, and to work closer to home, often even at home for pay or in a family enterprise for family profit. Furthermore, because of their assigned role as dependent members of the household, women tend to be relatively more active than men in non-market activities and in the informal sector.[4] They are considered by others and even by themselves as economically inactive; to receive less education, and thus more confined in occupations requiring lower skills and paying less; considered as secondary workers in their family enterprise even when they have equal responsibility; and, in times of economic downturn or structural adjustment, they are amongst the first dismissed from their paid jobs. In addition, women find it hard to break through the 'glass ceiling', which blocks their access to managerial or decision-making positions. Given structural constraints due to family responsibilities, women who are available and willing to work tend actively to seek work much less than men in the same situation and employers tend to be reluctant to employ women outside typically female occupations.[5]

Several theories have been provided to explain gender discrimination. Becker[6] conceives of the neo-classical theory of discrimination and refers to the tastes for discrimination prevailing among the employers. An employer who examines differences in productivity among different workers is likely to pay differently to different workers. Again wage difference could also be due to differences in investment on oneself. Greater investment on human capital would lead to greater productivity and, therefore, greater earnings. Another argument put forward by the neo-classical economists like Mincer and Polacheck[7] are that, women earn less than men because they have lower levels of human capital, viz. education, training, on-the-job training and, therefore, lower productivity. Cain,[8] who has tried to analyse gender discrimination on the basis of dummy variable approach, also expresses similar view. His opinion is that women during their course of development invest less than men in promoting their capabilities and human capital resource and, therefore, are paid less.

Another area of gender differentiation is the allocation of resources and benefits among the members of a household. It has been observed, for example, those women who are self-employed have more limited access to production resources than men, which lower their income.[9] Furthermore, women do not necessarily have control over their use of the resources available to them, nor do they necessarily reap the full benefits accruing from their efforts. Women and men's gender roles also determine their different needs and constraints. The degree to which women actually participate in and contribute to the production process is highly dependent on their marital status on whether they have small children, and on whether they have to care for other persons in their households. Men's participation in and contribution to the production process are also affected by these factors, but not in a constraining way.

While human capital theories propounded by Becker and Cain could be considered as the supply side approach to gender theories, the demand side theories explain that employers prefer men to women in certain types of jobs on the basis of their skill and sex. In general, women are excluded from various categories of job in the job market and even when employed are paid less due to differences in skill. An ILO study also revealed that women are considered to be high cost workers due to their high rate of irregularity, high turnover etc. and, therefore, are paid less and less preferred.[10]

Another theory, which explains labour market discrimination, is known as the Statistical Theory of Discrimination by Phelps,[11] where it has been shown that in the absence of knowledge of productivity and efficiency of a person, external factors like skin, colour, and sex determines the wages to be paid. Tilak[12] has also made a statistical measurement of "discrimination", where a macro model of sex discrimination from human capital formation and returns to it has been calculated. The result has shown that the level of unemployment at every level of education for women is higher.

Again studies by Madeshwaran and Shroff[13] and Frances[14] have shown that cultural and stereotyping of women's role, private and public divide decide to a large extent, the nature of work a woman ought to perform, and also controls women's access to quality employment and their performance in the labour market.

This has given rise to a growing body of feminist thought which on the one hand emphasizes the exclusion of women from the traditional male activities and institutions and a second body of feminist thought which emphasizes the devaluation of women's productive activities. It emerges, therefore, that gender bias exists or it fails to perceive the extent of traditional female activities or dispositions, which contribute to the economy, society or polity.[15]

The treatment of gender in standard economic analysis is used as a metaphor for a broader set of problems in economic theory. "Feminist Economics" could provide a better explanation of human behaviour over a broader range of economic situation. It thus becomes necessary to look at the participation of women from a feminist point of view.

Feminist economists express similar views like Shah[16], who feels that discrimination against female labour operates because in a labour surplus situation patriarchy or male dominant structure tends to prefer available men. And this is undoubtedly a fundamental question, which needs to be addressed.

## ECONOMIC TOPICS WHERE GENDER MATTERS

After decades of work aimed at achieving equality between men and women, after the adoption of numerous international resolutions and instruments and after the passage of national legislation seeking to attain this goal, it seems that there has been progress towards the elimination of sex discrimination in employment. In general, women's working conditions have improved, as has legal environment for creating greater equality, job mobility has increased, wage gaps have narrowed access to education has become easier and work schedules are more flexible.[17] All these factors have contributed to a lessening of the constraints affecting female job-seekers and workers. Questions remain, however, as to the evidence of improvement.

### Labour Force Participation

The labour force participation rate is an indicator of the overall level of labour market activity and its breakdown by sex and age group provides a profile of the distribution of the economically active population within the country.

It is calculated by expressing the number of persons in the labour force as a percentage of the working-age population.

In every country for which information is available, women are less likely than men to participate in the labour force. This reflects the fact that demographic, social, legal and cultural trends and norms determine whether or not women's activities are regarded as economic, with the result that women experience greater difficulty obtaining entry to the labour market than do men. Furthermore, in addition to overcoming the numerous educational, institutional and cultural barriers, which may prevent them from gaining access to the labour market, most women must also deal with the competing demands of housework and childcare.

Unlike men's labour force participation rates, which are high in all countries, there is great cross-country variation in women's rates.[18] Women's low labour force participation rates can be attributed to cultural factors. In some countries for example, the education of young women and women's work outside the home are often discouraged, owing to strict sex segregation for reasons of religion and marriage ability. Cultural practices and high fertility rates also play a large role in limiting women's economic opportunities. In developing countries, it is women's large share in agricultural work that accounts for their high labour force participation.

For majority of countries, the gap between women and men's labour force participation rates narrowed between 1980 and 1997. This stemmed both from declining male rates and from rising female rates. Decreasing employment in the male-dominated industrial sector may have led to a reduction in the labour force activity of older men.[19] The increase in women's labour force participation reflects, among other things, their rise in educational levels; the growth of the service sector, which includes industries in such areas as health care and retailing where women have particularly high representation and changing norms and laws concerning women's economic roles.

While economic development often brings about an increase in women's labour force participation, the question of whether women stake a claim to their country's growing wealth ultimately depends on that country's commitment to women's economic equality with men. This commitment is reflected in anti-discrimination policies with respect to work, property and contracts, policies to assist families in meeting their responsibilities, and policies to ensure a minimum living wage and decent working conditions.

**Flexibility of Female Occupations**

It seems clear that women's responsibility for housework and child care affects the types of jobs many women prefer, since job flexibility in terms of hours (or part-time jobs) and relatively easy entry/exit/re-entry enables women to combine work and family responsibilities more easily. On this gender theories and neo-classical theories agree.

However, there are two possible reasons why female occupations tend to be flexible in terms of hours and labour turnover. It could be that women gravitate towards occupations with these characteristics (either because of women preferences and characteristics and/or because employers prefer to employ women in these occupations) as explained by economic theory.[20] Or it could be that occupations become 'female', because of the sort of sex stereotyping with flexible working conditions emerging as a consequence of the fact that these are "female" occupations.

Although neo-classical economic theory holds that the preferences of women and employers are responsible for the concentration of women in flexible occupations, feminist theory does not support such an unequivocal conclusion, since both the possibilities noted above are consistent with it.[21] While family responsibilities can be expected to increase women's preferences for flexible occupations, the stereotyping of certain work as suitable for women can be expected to affect the types of occupation open to them.

The empirical analysis provides evidence indicating a high degree of consistency between the sex stereotyping of an occupation and the feminine stereotypes. It supports the conclusion that the flexibility and low pay associated with many typical 'female' occupations are due, to a large extent, to the fact that these are 'female' occupations. There is no reason to consider any occupation as inherently either more or less flexible.

**Equal Pay for Work of Equal Value**

In a number of countries legislation now requires equal pay for women performing work of equal value or of comparable worth to that performed by men in the same establishment. The aim is to prevent management, or trade unions and management acting together in collective bargaining from discriminating against women in female-dominated jobs by fixing lower wage levels for them.

In the post-independent India we had series of laws passed for the upliftment of women. The legislations have been brought out in order to give equal rights and privileges with men, eliminate discriminations against women, remove inequality between the sexes, and remove external barriers coming in the way of their self-realization and development.[22] Equal Remuneration Act of 1976 guarantees women equal pay for equal work. The Constitution of India guarantees certain fundamental rights and freedoms such as protection of life and personal liberty. Indian women are the beneficiaries of these rights in the same manner as the Indian men. The constitutional recognition of equal status for women and progressive legal enactments has undoubtedly empowered Indian women with judicial equality.

It has been established that female-dominated jobs or occupations are paid relatively lower wages than male-dominated and so that both men and women in an occupation are paid less resulting thereby the greater is the proportion of women employed in that occupation.[23] This crowding effect is more marked for men than for women. Average pay for both men and women in one occupation might be lower relative to average pay in occupations with a larger proportion of male workers, but within each occupation the crowding hypothesis should have no impact on the relative pay of men and women within that occupation. Discrimination theory seeks to explain whether, and if so why, employers choose not to employ women in certain jobs where they could have the same value of marginal product as men and presumably at wages lower than those men are currently paid, despite the probable concomitant increase in effective or acceptable labour supply and reduction in wages of both men and women.

It is necessary a matter of judgment whether two jobs are of comparable worth or requires the same skills and abilities. An element of subjective or value judgment will always be involved and on occasion the application of comparable worth analysis means imposing one set of values for the components of different jobs dissimilar to the values adopted by the persons who set the original pay levels.

Economic theory would conclude that in the absence of any market imperfections or demand-side discrimination, the pay gap between men and women with the same value of marginal product in the same location would be zero. Even in the highly restrictive case, however, a comparison of male and female pay may not be sufficient to establish the existence of discrimination.[24] There can be real differences in the value of marginal products of men and women doing the same work, this has long been recognized as typically true for jobs, which require physical strength. The presence of an occupational wage gap can, therefore, only be regarded as a first indication that wage discrimination may be in practice against women.

## LABOUR THEORIES

The operation of a market in a capitalist economy tied to private concentration of ownership of productive enterprise is essentially exploitative. The purpose of production is to ensure that the cost of production including the cost of labour is exceeded by the value of the product. This surplus value over cost is what goes to ownership that is the capitalist. The resultant effect is a chain of inequality and poverty. This is reflected in a hierarchy at work, in earning and in society.

Stratification in the labour market is justified because the employers pay women workers less than others, and creates group of flexible low paid workers who can be moved in and out of employment as and when needed.

Based on the broad ideas of feminist school several theories have emerged in recent times in an attempt at capturing the experience of women in the labour market. These theories on labour market, focusing attention to the status of women, emphasize on diverse aspects of discrimination in the labour market on the basis of gender.[25] For instance, according to the Neo-classicalists and the Marxists, family constitutes the basis for women's position in the labour market. The entry of women into the labour market as well as their earnings and status is determined by their status in the society. On the other hand the radicals and the advocates of the dual system theories, who come under the institutional labour market school, consider the political factors to play the dominant role in determining the role of women in the labour market. Another group of economists assign cultural factors, i.e., the process of socialization prior to the entry into the labour market, which determines status and position in the labour market.[26]

However, the feminist economists consider patriarchy to be the only factor, which plays a crucial role in governing the position of women in the labour market. They emphasize the need for understanding gender relations and their interconnections with other social relations. Feminist argues that it is women who is trapped in the stratification process and is the most vulnerable resource in the labour market. Accordingly different labour theories have been discussed to show whether gender-neutral treatment exists for women in the labour market.

**Human Capital Model**

Neo-classical economies assume that workers and employers are rational and that labour markets function efficiently. According to this theory, workers seek out the best paying jobs after taking into consideration their own personal endowments (e.g., education, experience), constraints (e.g., young child to take care of), and preferences (e.g., a pleasant work environment). Employers try to maximize profits by maximizing productivity and minimizing costs to the extent possible, but because of competition and efficient labour markets, employers pay workers their marginal product. Neo-classicalists argue that since men spend more time in the labour market, they acquire greater experience and hence the difference between men and women in terms of the job status as well as wage differentiation. Due to their household responsibilities women choose those jobs, which require less time and skill in the labour market.

**Dual Labour Market Theory**

Institutional and labour market segmentation theories also rely on well-established economic thought and neo-classical logic. Their starting point is the assumption that institutions, such as unions and large enterprises, play an important role in determining who is hired, fired and promoted, and how much they are paid. Institutional theories also begin with the assumption that labour markets are segmented in certain ways. And while each labour market segment may function according to neo-classical theory, it is difficult for workers to pass from one segment to another.

The best known is dual labour market theory, this theory, associated with the name of Hartmann,[27] attempts to combine the Marxist and the feminist views to examine labour market discrimination. In other words, capitalism combined with patriarchy is the factor responsible for the segregation. In the patriarchal society, men accentuate this segregation by keeping the higher paid jobs for themselves. This is possible mainly due to better organizing power of men in comparison to women. Consequently continuance of discrimination benefits capital as well as patriarchy simultaneously. Women, therefore, are pushed into jobs of low status requiring less skill and less pain. They are, therefore, expected to bear a greater degree of responsibility in a patriarchal system. Though critics point out that analytical separation between capitalism and patriarchy is extremely difficult but for the purpose of examining gender discrimination the labour market theory highlights a crucial angle for such discrimination.

**Cultural Theories of Labour Market**

Rubery and Tarling, Openheimer and Mathhaei, the main proponents of this theory argue that since the social and cultural values of women differ from that of men, the position and status of women too based on this socialization process too differ from that of men. Jobs are chosen as well as assigned on the basis of their masculine or feminine behavioural traits. Tradition imbibed in culture is also accepted as an important determinant of the difference of status in the job market. Consequently the theory assigns factors outside the labour market to play the pivotal role in the determination of status in the labour market.

In this connection, several studies maintain that males and females themselves prefer to maintain sex segregation in the labour market.[28] None of them prefer to venture into domain of the others, nor do they encourage entry of the members of the other sex into their type of jobs. This theory, however, provides only a partial explanation of the factors responsible for segregation of labour market on gender line. However, the basic idea of the theory goes against the tenets of feminist since they consider such ideas to further strengthen the labour market segregation based on cultural division of the society on gender line.

**Statistical Discrimination Theory**

Another economic theory related to labour market segmentation is the statistical discrimination theory. This is based on the assumption that there are differences on average, in the productivity, skills, experience, etc., of distinct groups of workers (such as men and women), and high search and information costs associated with recruitment and promotion decisions. In such circumstances, it is argued, it is rational for employers to discriminate against groups of workers (such as women) when differences, on average, between the abilities of persons from different groups (e.g., men and women) cost less to sustain than the decision-making costs associated with identifying suitable individual workers of either sex.[29] Statistical discrimination theory thus provides and explanation for how some occupations are almost entirely for male even though many individual women have greater ability, more education, etc. than many individual men.

**Female Marginalisation**

The basic idea of this theory is based on the contribution of a number of writers (Eisenstein, Hartmann and Varghese), who are proponents of Marxist and socialist feminist school as well as radical school. The idea of the theory emerges from the capitalist system of modern production process, which progressively marginalized women from production. In contrast radical feminists[30] consider patriarchy, a feature of the biological aspect of man rather than the system of production, to be behind marginalization. These theories thereby have attempted to integrate the system of capitalism and patriarchy to be governing the type and nature of marginalisation in the labour market.

Feminists who have assigned cultural and sociological factors for female marginalisation in work place have enriched the marginalisation thesis further. However, the difference lies in their perception of the process. It will, therefore, be pertinent to highlight the various forms of female marginalisation.

First, the female work participation rate falls due to the exclusion of women from productive employment and thereby a concomitant fall in their respective share of wage and salary. Secondly, marginalisation may imply pushing the women workers to the margin in the labour market with unimportant jobs. Consequently there may be overcrowding of women in jobs at the margin.

Marginalisation thesis, therefore, for the first time focuses attention to a variety of factors responsible for work participation in the labour market, which is totally biased against women as against one factor as accepted in the other theories. According to this theory there are two labour markets, the primary and secondary labour markets.

The primary labour market comprises of unionized or professional job, with high wages, benefits, good working conditions and chances for advancement. It is generally close to external competition or highly limited by qualifications. Man predominates in this job.

The secondary labour market is characterized by the low wage with few benefits and open to external competition. It is here that women are marked by their presence in significant numbers. Women operate in this sector as part-time with unstable jobs in this market. The large pool of unemployed workers keep wages down in this labour market and poverty, low income, low status is generally associated with the situation in the labour market.

### CONCEPT OF WORK PARTICIPATION

Man is a social being. His very existence in the society evolves through a process of participation, be it economic or non-economic. Participation, according to standard dictionary is to take part and women along with men have been actively taking part in various activities. However, these activities are basically classified into two types—one that is reproductive and the other productive activities. Reproductive activities refer to the recreation of same species or of the same kind[31]. Productive activities are concerned with the process of producing goods, which are again subdivided into subsistence production and market related production. Subsistence production refers to production of goods and commodities, which have, exchange value. It is in this context that the women participation rate particularly in the economic sphere in the market economy assumes importance.

Participation rate means the contribution made by the women by taking an active part in the economic activity of a nation. Generally, this contribution is measured in monetary terms so that one can contribute to the GDP of a nation. The female work participation rates determines the percentage of women working which necessarily helps to indicate whether they are fully employed drawing wages or marginally employed with minimum wage or remain underpaid.

Studies by Banerjee[32] and Mitra[33] have shown that women engage themselves both in the creation of subsistence output, as well as products to which market value can be assigned. They perform the dual role of bread earner and child rearing, between productive and unproductive work and paid employment in both the organized and unorganised sectors. In spite of that, a major proportion of productive work remains unrecognized and under-valued leading to an under-estimation of the valuable contribution of many women outside the mainstream of economic activity. Absence of assigning monetary value to such contribution of women has led to the unrecognition and under-recognition of women participation in economic activity and thus in the overall economic progress of a nation. This tendency prevents the women from earning any remunerative income in proportion to their contribution in the economic life of a nation. Woman, therefore, suffers from under-valuation of their economic status since the overall status of a person is associated with the income earning capabilities of a person.

Though women labour force participation is an important determinant to indicate a woman's status, however, to assess her overall well-being we cannot restrict the scope only to levels or types of employment. This could perhaps provide only a myopic vision to question about women's overall status. During the early stages of development, most studies indicate towards the U-shaped hypothesis, which explains that women's participation falls in the earliest stages of economic development, and rise again with modernization and advancement of the economy. This is generated in the economy through female empowerment and education and the rising demand from women services in the tertiary sectors.[34]

While the U-shaped curve describes a general pattern, there are many other factors such as fertility rates, child morbidity rates, cultural factors etc., which also influence the extent of labour force participation especially women. In matriarchal societies, where women's participation in any form of economic activity is readily accepted, it is possible to show that neither in the rural or urban areas does fertility, nor the presence of children, nor the existence of any other male earning member in the family makes any significant difference in the participation of women.

In India and States and within regions, there has been much diversity in the structure of the population. Across regions, the patterns and trends of the characteristics of population, growth rates, age structure, infant mortality, social expenditure vary considerably and each of these factors are exclusively responsible to some extent in determining the participation of women in the workforce. Though it shall not be possible to comprehend all these factors or variables within our study, yet an analysis and corelation of these factors with the participation rate would help us to highlight the socio and human factors lying behind the work participation of women in the workforce.

## CONCLUSION

Women's movement and feminist concerns have in recent years brought into focus that the problems of women workers are not only economic but also social. Through the works of the feminist researchers and activists, a comprehensive coverage in dealing with this woman component workforce has been brought into focus. Their studies have revealed that at the heart of most of the situation adversely affecting the social development prospects of women are strongly prevailing ideologies, which differentiate between women and men to the disadvantage of women. A different perception of women means that different roles, rights regimes access to services and so on. What is, therefore, necessary is to raise the social development prospect for women through education and awareness raising and gender gap addressed through education and legislation policies and programmes aimed at achieving greater equality.

With increasing competition across the globe, it is increasingly important for countries to make efficient use of their resources. What could be a more important source of labour market inefficiency than extensive segmentation of male and female workers? With the impact of women liberation movement, and an increasing participation of women in the labour force and in public life, the most important thing is to create equal opportunities for men and women. Policy makers need to address more seriously the inequality of labour market opportunities and its effect on men and women. A wide variety of policies and programmes is needed—for example, facilitating policies to reduce the burden on women of family responsibilities; consciousness-raising programmes to remove gender stereotypes and prejudices; educational policies to bring about greater gender equality in schooling and training, especially with respect to opening access to non-traditional occupations for both men and women; and equal opportunity and affirmative action policies, especially those opening up new opportunities for men and women. Action is required on all these fronts to reduce occupational segregation between men and women with benefits not only for the present workforce and economy but also for the future.

## NOTES

1. Gunderson, M. (1989): 'Male and Female Wage Differential and Policy Responses', *Journal of Economic Literature*, Vol. 24, No.1.
2. Sloane, P.J. (1985): 'Discrimination in the Labour Market' in D. Carline *et al.* (eds.) *Labour Economics*, Harloro Longman
3. Leftwich H. Richard, Ansel and Sharp M. (1984), *Economics of Social Issues*, Business Publications, Plano, Texas.
4. Jhabwala, R. and R.K. Subramanyam (2000): *The Unorganised Sector: Work Security and Social Protection*, Sage Publications, New Delhi.
5. Mitra, A. *et al.* (1979): *The Status of Women, Household and Non-household Economic Activity*, Allied Publishers, New Delhi.
6. Becker, G. (1964): *Human Capital: A Theoretical and Empirical Analysis with Special Reference to Education*, National Bureau of Economic Research, New York.
7. Mincer, J. and Polacheck, S.W. (1974): 'Family Investments in Human Capital, Earnings of Women', *Journal of Political Economy*.

8. Cain, M.T. (1980): *The Economic Activities of Children in a Village in Bangladesh,* Rural Household Studies in Asia, Singapore University Press.
9. Anker, Richard (2002): 'Theories of Occupational Segregation by Sex', in Martha Fetherolf Loutfi (ed.), *Women, Gender and Work,* ILO, Geneva.
10. Rothbeck, S. and Sarthi, A. (1999): 'Gender Based Segregation in the Indian Labour Market', *Indian Journal of Labour Economics,* Vol. 42, No. 4.
11. Phelps, E.S. (1972): 'The Statistical Theory of Racism and Sexism', *American Economic Review,* Vol. 62, No. 4.
12. Tilak, Jandhyala B. G. (1980): 'Education and Labour Market Discrimination', *Indian Journal of Industrial Relations,* Vol. XVI, 1, July 1980.
13. Madheswaran, S. and Shroff, Sangeeta (2000) : 'Education Employment and Earnings for Scientific and Technical Workforce in India : Gender Issues', *The Indian Journal of Labour Economics,* Vol. 43, No. 1
14. Frances, I. Jeanne (1994): 'Working and Living for the Family, Gender, Work and Education', *Indian Journal of Gender Studies,* Vol. 1, No. 1.
15. Folbre M. and Nelson, J. (1993): 'Introduction: the Social Construction of Economics and the Social Construction of Gender', in *Beyond Economic Man-Feminist Theory and Economics,* Chicago University Press, Chicago.
16. Shah, M.S. (1975): 'Wages and Employment of Women in India', *Indian Labour Journal,* 16, No. 2.
17. Bell, C.S. (2002): 'Data on Race, Ethnicity and Gender: Caveats for the User', in Martha Fetherolf Loutfi (ed.), *Women Gender and Work,* ILO, Geneva.
18. Dholakia, B.H. and Dholakia, R.H. (1978): 'Inter-State Variation in Female Labour Force Participation Rates', *Indian Journal of Labour Economics,* Vol. XX, No. 4.
19. Durand, J.D. and Miller, A.R. (1973): *Labour Force and Economic Development,* Population Study Centre, University of Pennsylvania (Mimeo).
20. Gupta, R.N. (1984): 'Correlates of Female Participation in Economic Activity', *Indian Labour Journal,* Vol. 25, No. 3, March.
21. Folbre, N. (ed.) (1993): *Beyond Economic Man-Feminist Theory and Economics,* Chicago University Press, Chicago.

22. Ghosh, B. and Mukhopadhya, S.K. (1984): 'Displacement of the Female in the Indian Labour Force', *EPW*, Vol. XIX, No. 47, November.

23. Derek Robinson (2002): 'Differences in Occupational Earnings by Sex', in Martha Fetherolf Loutfi (ed.), *Women, Gender and Work*, ILO, Geneva.

24. Ghosh, B. and Mukhopadhaya Sudhir (1990): 'Share of Women in Income Employment and Work: A Macro-Micro Economic Inquiry', Samya Shakti, *A Journal of Women's Studies*, Vols. IV and V.

25. Gulati, Leela (1975): 'Sex Discrimination in Work and Wages', *Social Scientist*, Vol. 4 (4-5).

26. Gunderson, M. (1989): Male and Female Wage Differential and Policy Responses, *Journal of Economic Literature*, Vol. 24, No. 1.

27. Hartmann Heidi (1969): 'The Family as the Locus of Gender, Class and Political Struggle: The Example of Housework' in Anne C. Herrmann and Abigail J. Stewart, Westview Press, USA.

28. Rothbeck, S. and Sarthi, A. (1999): 'Gender Based Segregation in the Indian Labour Market', *Indian Journal of Labour Economics*, Vol. 42, No. 4.

29. Sloane, P.J. (1985): 'Discrimination in the Labour Market' in D. Carline *et al.* (eds.) *Labour Economics*, Harloro Longman.

30. Benn, S.I. and Gans, G.F. (1983): *Public and Private in Social Life* (ed.), St. Martins Press, New York

31. Mitra, A. *et al.* (1979): *The Status of Women, Household and Non-household Economic Activity*, Allied Publishers, New Delhi.

32. Banerjee Nirmala (1995): 'Women's Rights and Development Policies in India', *The Administrator*, Vol. XL, July–September

33. Mitra, A. (1995): *Labour and Development*, Vol. 1, No. 1, July–December, V.V. Giri National Labour Institute.

34. Paukert, Liba (1984): *The Employment and Unemployment of Women in OECD Countries*, OECD, France.

# 3

# REVIEW OF LITERATURE

In this chapter, a modest attempt has been made to discuss the varied literatures that have relevance to our topic on Gender and Development with special emphasis on female work participation. This has been a humble attempt on the part of the researcher to examine different studies, which brings into focus the increasing attention that is being paid to understand the economic role of women in society.

Literatures on women's work have been divided into the following categories :

1. Women's work a theoretical explanation.
2. Regional variations of women's work in India
   (a) Economic factors
   (b) Socio-cultural factors
   (c) Technological factors.
3. Occupational segregation/discrimination.
4. Government policies.
5. Legal redressal policies.
6. Conclusion.

## THEORIES ON WOMEN'S WORK

Several theoretical explanations have been provided to explain women's involvement of work outside the home both in developed and underdeveloped countries. The most important question taken up for theoretical explanation was why women go for paid employment and why does inequality of pay exist.

According to Mincer,[1] whether women will go for paid employment or not will rest upon the effect of income or price. A cross-section study shows that women's work participation and husband's income are inversely related,[2] while a time-series study shows the opposite.[3] The contradiction is supposed to have been resolved by showing that when income of the family increases, women prefer more leisure, i.e. the substitution effect is greater than the negative income effect.

According to Becker ,[4] in the family production process, women hire men as bread earner because men in terms of their capabilities and skill earn more than women in the market and men hire women to bear and rear the children as women possess the superior skill for this task. Mincer and Polachek[5] explain women's low pay in the labour market on the argument of Human Capital Theory. Earnings command in the labour market depend on an individual productivity, which is dependent on a person's innate abilities to acquire characteristics like education, training, work experiences etc., summarized as human capital. As compared to men, women invest less than men in human capital because they spend proportionately less time in the labour force due to social and family commitments. Due to lack of accumulation of work experiences, human capital depreciates and, therefore, earning gap is automatically created.

## REGIONAL VARIATIONS OF WOMEN WORK IN INDIA

In India, the participation of women varies from region to region and also between rural and urban areas. Even among states and among districts wide variation in female participation rates are observed even for the most developed and developing countries.

Krishnan[6] in a study of district level participation of working women in certain selected states has categorized different States like Andhra Pradesh, Tamil Nadu, Karnataka, Madhya Pradesh and Maharashtra, which formed the largest single contiguous area of high proportion of both men and women workers. The notable causes underlined have been the following using enumeration and cross comparison of census data:

(a) The absence of strict taboos against female participation in work.

(b) The primitive subsistence economy requiring participation of maximum number of family members.

(c) The setting up of various industrial plants, which has resulted in a large participation of women from within the household to work as daily or contractual labourers.

Chandra[7] in his study of some major States has shown that some of the lowest participation of women workers is to be observed in States like Jammu and Kashmir, Punjab, Rajasthan, Gujarat, Uttar Pradesh, Bihar, West Bengal and Orissa. The main causes attributed to are:

(a) Low female work participation rate.

(b) There is a strong bias against female participation outside home in states like Jammu and Kashmir being Muslim dominated.

(c) Social taboos prevent women to participate in economically productive activities in States like Bihar, Uttar Pradesh, and Rajasthan.

Though the studies both by Gupta and Chandra have highlighted some important variables, which may be attributed for high or low proportion of workers but the effect of these variables are not correlated to work participation rate for women. It was based on empirical case study. Krishnan[8] has analysed the pattern of work participation rate of women of North-West India during the period 1971-1991 correlating the proportion of workers to certain explanatory variables and for this purpose the statistical tool of zero-order correlation was applied.

**Economic Factors**

The pace of development is closely associated with female labour force participation rates. Whyte and Whyte[9] observed that participation of females in certain types of gainful employment does increase with economic development, but beyond the point, this increase fails to compensate for a decline of employment in the more traditional industries. Thus, the long-run effect of industrialization, according to Whyte, may be to raise the overall rate of female labour force, but the short-run effect may be to lower it.

Boserup[10] observed that in the early stages of industrialization, in spite of the expansion of modern sector there is a fall in the female participation rates because women fail to find employment in this sector to compensate for the relative or absolute decline of those sectors, employing women in greater proportions. The overall decline in FWR would continue, according to Boserup, till the modern sectors become so great relative to other sectors that the positive changes can offset the decline elsewhere due to the structural changes in the economy.

Nath's[11] study brings into focus the economic necessity, institutional restrictions in employment and the nature and type of employment that are available for a woman. Major finding of his study was industry-wise analysis of female-male ratios showing that women are represented primarily in the traditional, household sector of each industry and their participation is low in the modern organised sector. The study also forecasts that economic development, if not accompanied simultaneously with employment opportunities in the organised sector and similar avenues in the rural sector, will be followed by a progressive decline in the work participation rate of women until countervailing influences come into play.

Mitra, Srimany and Pathak[12] analyzing the status of women in household and non-household economic activity in India have raised two very vital points. First, the mean participation sex ratio is quite low in India and this is enough reason to understand the very low position that women occupy in employment *vis-à-vis* men. Secondly, wherever women are in employment they are mainly in very low earning sectors of the economy demanding strenuous work and in low skill and low technology sectors of low productivity. This is also supported in the study of Kalpagam,[13] where she has shown that a considerable number of women workers are engaged in the informal sector performing piece-rate work, casual jobs and petty trading. But the significance of their work in the economic survival is grossly underestimated.

Neetha[14] mentions certain positive factors, which, according to her emerge from female labour force participation. They are as follows:

1. Women become increasingly involved in economic activities outside the household, the status of women in the society will increase which in turn leads to an increase in the social value of a girl child.
2. Participation in remunerative employment increases the return to investment in girls.
3. Economic independence also raises the status of the girl child within the family.

**Social Factors**

Social resources which increase women's participation are education, employment, access to earned income, participation in decision-making so as to expand their capabilities, achieve empowerment and establish more equal gender relations.

Among the various social factors that have been examined, Jayaweera[15] has tried to show a relation between education and employment opportunities for women. In his study Jayaweera has shown that there does not always appear a positive relationship between education and employment. Some newly industrialised nations have witnessed women being vulnerable to displacement in the change from labour to skill intensive industries because of lack of relevant skills.

The relation between work participation rate and educational level is rather mixed. For example, in the industrialized countries highly educated female suffers less unemployment. On the other hand, in agro-based economies and especially in India the correlation is rather contrasted. Reddy[16] found from a cross-sectional analysis of 1971 Census data that participation rates were higher for illiterate females in both the rural and urban areas than for those with middle school and ordinary graduated females, although a steep rise is seen in those females' educational level of matric and above. While some researchers found that although illiterate women form part of the workforce in greater proportion than the literate ones, but within the literate group highly educated women take part in economic activities in greater proportion.

King and Hill[17] in their study indicated that female schooling is considered to be more significant as compared to male schooling for certain social outcomes such as fertility, child health and infant mortality. These aspects could be more effectively dealt with through educating the girl child, by making them conscious and aware of these factors. Schultz[18] also suggests that the economic gains from women's education are generally high as those from men's education.

Monohar[19] finds that the socio-economic situation, non-implementation of relevant laws and regulations, ineffective performance of government policies had direct bearing both on the women workers and the status of women. Her study examines further that social conditions continue to be anti-women in character. The economic condition is characterized by class structure and relations, which alienate women from the mainstream of development. And it is this deterioration of socio-economic conditions that have a direct bearing on women's participation rate.

Ivan and Hoffman[20] have pointed out three different factors that affect women's employment: (a) Specific and general attitude of family and community; (b) opportunities for employment; and (c) the male members or husband's attitude to women's work which determines to a great extent the nature and type of work a woman would do.

In a similar study, Broadbun *et al.*[21] argue that apart from the social and income status, which influence a woman's decision to work, factors such as woman's education, her family's literacy level, size of her family and her stage in the life cycle are important predictors of her probability of entering the labour market.

**Technological Factors**

Agro-economists and rural sociologists in India conducted a number of studies in different parts of the country to find out the impact of introduction of new technology on women labour force participation and its consequences on their status. One set of studies[22] depicts the positive role of new technology so far as the status of rural women is concerned. The second, however, indicates that the introduction of new technology has reduced the status of women to utter dependency. These two perspectives become very clear if we look at the results of different studies, which have shown varying results on the status of women.

Krishna[23] in his study in Vidharbha compared the level of female labour utilisation in crop production with traditional technology and modern technology. He came to the conclusion that new technology has given more working days and employment opportunities to women. The finding further indicated that in the case of male workers, there was a shift from agricultural to non-agricultural occupations while an increasing number of female workers found employment on farms. Similarly, studies conducted in Punjab by Chandra[24] indicated that modernization of agriculture had resulted into increased employment per hectare of cultivated area for all kinds of female labour.

Sinha[25] in his studies in the States of Rajasthan, Madhya Pradesh and Kerala came to the conclusion that as a result of adoption of new technology in agriculture, female employment in absolute and relative sense has increased in agricultural operations. This also indicates that with the change in the technique of crop production, the workload of women has also increased.

Sharma and Singh[26] also observed that due to better irrigation facilities the cropping pattern was changed and shifted in favour of labour intensive crops. They concluded that due to irrigation, for all the crops, labour employment increased more than two-folds. This trend was higher in the case of female than male labourers.

Bardhan[27] found that with the out-migration of men, women were compelled to take over the farm management tasks. She also revealed that with the mechanization of agriculture and out-migration of male members, more than three-fourths of women workers were to make decisions relating to the choice of crops, technology, credit and marketing, in addition to household activities.

Banerjee[28] highlights the importance and magnitude of the economic role played by rural women through their active participation in various agricultural activities. She further indicated that women's role in agriculture is so significant that without them nothing can be done. It is for this reason that women in this region enjoy a relatively better position. As a consequence of modernization of agriculture, labour force participation of women has increased. This has provided them with an opportunity to have access to new knowledge, and women are now taking independent decisions relating to agricultural production and development thereby reducing the wage differential of men and women workers.

Gopalan[29] has focused an alarming point that in the near future the entry of women in the labour force is going to be in greater magnitude than before due to women's improvement in their educational status, greater awareness and increasing economic necessities. Agricultural sector, which has been the largest sector providing employment has also reached saturation point being inelastic to increasing production. The study focuses that, in the emerging situation, women need to be empowered with new modern skills with more technological inputs to increase productivity.

Similarly, the impact of technological development on women's employment has drawn the attention of various scholars. Ghosh and Mukhopadhyay[30] using various census and secondary sources of data have analysed the data on employment in India and have observed that there has been a drastic reduction in the number of women workers as well as their work participation rates.

Acharya[31] has shown that the decline in women's employment in modern organised industries is due to the development of industries along with a simultaneous growth of technology. Using refined tools for indicators of technical change such as capital accumulation and capital intensity, he analyses the shift in industrial structure over the period of 1950-1974. The findings of the study reveals that women gradually get displaced from the traditional jobs which has taken over by modern methods of production for which the women were neither trained nor considered for such jobs. Modernisation of limited segments of agriculture coupled with the disappearance of the household industries led to greater ruralisation of the population.

As distinct from the above historical explanation, some scholars have developed statistical models to explain variation in female work participation.

Through the use of census data, the paper by M.S. Fong[32] establishes the levels and changes in female labour participation rates for each of the three major ethnic groups in Malaya and Singapore between the period of 1921 and 1957. During this period, female labour force participation rates declined rapidly both inside and outside agricultural sector. The explanation for the finding is tested in multiple regression analysis. The results have shown that the best predictor of the overall level of female labour force participation is not the level of male labour force participation, or the sex ratio but the proportion of workers employed in agriculture.

In a set of exercise by Duvvury[33] it has been found that there has been a significant increase in the number and proportion of female agricultural wage labourers in many States. The reason cited are mainly two-fold: (a) the horizontal mobility of women workers form the non-agricultural labour groups and (b) the process of pauperization of rural households also influences women to enter into wage-employment force in India between 1961 and 1981. The study has been done by examining the changes in the sectoral distribution of female labour force in different States of India in 1961 to 1981.

Saksena[34] has undertaken the study to understand the inter-State disparities in female work participation, which has been found to be more glaring than male work participation rate. Two measures of inequality have been employed. The standard deviation and co-efficient of variation have been employed to highlight the effect of the social, economic and cultural variables which affects the work participation rate.

Most prominent is the work of Sunderam,[35] the principal contentions, found significant in a multivariate regression analysis are : (a) as the burden of household activity increases, the additional burden of participation in economic activity is hampered, (b) conventionally there exists a tendency for women to withdraw themselves from the workforce as solvency sets in, and (c) in the rural sector, access to self-employment creates a positive impact on the workforce participation of rural women.

There are a number of empirical studies conducted in different parts of India on rural women where the researchers have come to the conclusion that different developmental processes undertaken in rural India, have adversely affected them to the extent that their labour participation has decreased and their dependency increased.

The use of modern technology in agricultural production has adversely affected women's work participation. A number of studies have highlighted that women's work participation in agricultural production is not related to new technology or lack of it. On the other hand, work participation of women depends on cropping pattern, landholdings, income and caste status of the family.

## DISCRIMINATION

Discrimination is an area of keen interest of researchers. These studies observe that women are mainly engaged in low paid, low skilled and low productivity jobs in unorganised sectors. Papola and Sharma[36] found that women have less access to higher positions, and the employer's own attitude is a major factor contributing to women's low share of employment, which tend to place women in a secondary position and under subjugation to men.

Bell[37] was of the opinion that discrimination on pay differentials between men and women exists due to imperfection of market created by male monopoly power. When male workers are highly unionized they may dislike association with women at work where women gain access to supervisory roles. But critics point out that union would never support wage discrimination in the same occupation, as this would induce employers to hire female workers than males with the objective of minimizing cost.

The version of Becker[38] assumes competitive market conditions. Thurow[39] has raised objections against this competitive framework—the central proposition of which is that the discriminator must lose income if one wishes to discriminate. He develops an alternate taste for discrimination on the basis of social distance; by social distance he means that females should have a position, which is lower or subordinate to men. He differentiates between men and women for doing the same work and identifies several types of discrimination. He mentions about market discrimination that takes the form of salary differentials between men and women for doing the same work where on the basis of education, skill and capabilities, women are given jobs inferior to men.

Tilak[40] in her studies made an attempt to study sex discrimination using a macro model analysis. Discrimination is measured using statistical technique by establishing a relation between education, earnings-differentials and unemployment. The study shows that the incidence of unemployment at every level of education of women is higher, yet it failed to examine why variations in earnings among females cannot be attributed to discrimination in a setting of sexual segregation of markets. Similarly, Banerjee[41] through her explicit study has shown how women are confined to regular, monotonous, less skilled and low paid jobs due to differences in sex.

Unequal gender relations are less prominent among the social functions of the women of southern India with higher levels of participation rates and higher literacy rate. In all aspects of social standing women's position is better off. All these theories make it clear that discrimination mainly comes from two sources: (i) market and (ii) human imperfections which are due to imperfect knowledge, immobility of resources and imperfect competition. Human imperfections are revealed in the tastes and preferences that some people have for discrimination, which manifests itself in the form of wage, employment, occupational and price discrimination. But the social and economic cost of discrimination is both individual and social in nature. Gender and segregation at social, political and cultural levels provide congenial ambience and environment for preparatory grounds of discrimination which eventually culminate into sexual division of labour and wage discrimination and unequal participation at various levels of decision-making process.[42]

## GOVERNMENT POLICY PRESCRIPTIONS

The National Labour Organisation has recommended a strict vigilance over all the industrial units directing them to follow all relevant provisions contained in the legislations regarding safety and welfare of all workers including the women workers. International Labour Organisation is also of the view that favourable working conditions are necessary to improve the performance of the workers and see to it that the workers work better without stress and strain. Productivity and efficiency of the workers are directly related to favourable working conditions.[43]

Kingdon,[44] in her work on the labour market, has attempted to examine the gender gap that exists and suggested some policy prescriptions to reduce the gender inequality especially in education. Two important policy prescriptions have been suggested: (1) encouragement of women's education and (2) policies to put an end to sex discrimination. These policies if implemented would raise the rates of returns to women's education and they would be mutually reinforcing. To promote increased participation Kingdon[45] and Whyte and Whyte[46] in their works mention about the existence of various international activities, which have been developed over the years basically to make women economically self-reliant and empowered.

Devi,[47] in her study of Status and Employment of Women has found that the condition of women in India is largely dependent to the extent of economic independence. She further suggests that from the policy point of view, there is a need to replace the traditional value system based on gender inequality with a more egalitarian system. The strategy needs to be focused on education, employment, and health and she is in favour of full revolution and revamping of the Panchayati Raj system with more democratic powers assigned to women.

There have also been quite a few evaluatory studies on projects favouring women's economic improvement. Some of these studies worth mentioning are by Jain,[48] Krishna Raj[49] and Nayak.[50] All these studies have voiced the general opinion that women policies need to work beyond 'charity concepts' and projects through which women could exercise control over their enterprises and resources.

Similar views regarding the ineffectiveness of the policy plans to remove the inequalities that have affected women more adversely than men have also been reported in the Draft National Perspective Plan (1988-2000). Therefore, the gaps between the analysis of problems and recommendation for needed measures have been approached through expansion of participatory opportunities through total cooption and total perspective for national development.

Bagchi[51] contributes in a significant way to understand policies regarding equal opportunity, sexual equality, positive discrimination and affirmative action. She argues that labelling women under a broad category 'women' actually deceives the problems of hierarchy within a subgroups defined in general terms merely by biological identification. Therefore, policy-makers need to be representative of social groups for whom affirmative action needs to be addressed. She refers to the case of Sweden, where gender equality and gender neutrality, which, as a joint package, may have contributed towards individual freedom and individual right in the workplace, but in reality, created further handicaps for women. Amendments in the legal structure exists but with dominance of positive discrimination. However, in recent years, creation of awareness and access to education has witnessed an implementation of these policies to the benefit of women.

## LEGAL MEASURES

Desai,[52] in her work on Gender Role in the Constitution has made an attempt to discover the underlying principles of gender role in the Constitution. Her study reveals that the Constitution does not contain a category of 'women', to which one may refer for understanding the position of women as provided in the Constitution. While Part III and Part IV of the Constitution dealing with the Fundamental Rights and Directive Principles of State Policy, do consider women as equal citizens, and fundamentally deny inequality in personal, economic, educational and other basic rights. She strongly comments that the injustice inflicted to women in many ways leads one to believe that the Constitution has been supportive of gender bias of the State.

Dixit[53] also mentioned the various provisions enshrined in our Constitution which protects or safeguards the rights of women. The Article 1 of the Universal Declaration of Human Rights of the United Nations says that all human beings are born free and equal in dignity and right and Article 2 of the Declaration emphasizes that everyone is entitled to all the rights and freedoms without distinction of sex. Dixit mentions the convention on the elimination of all forms of discrimination against women which stresses on the fact that discrimination against women violates the principles of equality of rights and respect for human dignity and acts as an impediment to participate with men on an equal footing. It deprives not only the women of fully utilizing their potentialities but also is a loss of productive and qualitative human resources.

Mukhopadhya[54] states that while the movement for gender justice inevitably gravitates towards legal reforms, the experience with law and various legal institutions that exist has led to disenchantment with the potential of law as an instrument of social transformation. The author has made an attempt to deliberate on four specific issues such as rights and laws from a feminist perspective, women's health as a legal right, and the institutionalization of women, which deals with issue of confinement of women in prisons, protection homes etc. where the closed nature of our institutions has not enabled these women to live in dignity and respect. Violence against women within and outside home has also been discussed against the main role of the Indian Penal Code. Jointly the study has attempted to reveal that most of the legislation that are implemented are not gender specific and, therefore, have stressed the need for the importance of Women's Organisation Samities and Non-Governmental Organisation (NGO) which may go a long way as support organization for empowering women.

Sarkar[55] examines the existence of prevalence of legislation, which has been emphasized by the Indian social reformers, right from the British days with the objective of fulfilling the constitutional mandate of equality of sexes, bringing equality in opportunity to employment. In her paper, she probes into various Acts, which have been implemented from time to time. However, the paper deals mainly with the reinterpretation of the Constitution and the role of the judiciary in matters of social relation such as marriage, rape etc. But the study has been able to highlight a central aspect that Women's Movement and legal process had been able to bring into light the anomalies in the social structure during the last two decades. The study has also shown that Women's Movement of various kinds has been active in demanding enforcement and implementation of the laws in favour of removing the disparity towards women. But laws relating to women's employment and wages have not received any detailed analysis in her study.

## CONCLUSION

The analysis of the interrelationship of the various studies dealing with women's work shows that there has undoubtedly been a proliferation of women's studies and an increased awareness to evolve emancipation and equality among women in all fields. A common thread, which runs in all these studies, is the recognition that exclusion of women from the various development processes actual or effective is one of the major causes for gender inequality and women's powerlessness.

In the process of documenting empirical evidence of women's work, useful categories like family production, market production and housework have emerged. Accordingly various methods have been improved upon such as 'imputation technique', 'time allocation method', 'cross-sectional study' to deal with women's work.

The comparative low participation of female with respect to male has been extensively dealt with through Census, NSS and Cross-sectional and Regional Studies. Micro-studies have mainly focused on the rural women's work based on different aspects like duration of employment, differentials in earnings, division of labour and sex-based segregation of jobs, impact of cropping pattern and examination of women's employment and income. On the other hand macro-studies have concentrated on subjects relating to changes in FWPR due to definitional changes, structural changes and policy changes. New areas of research have focused on women in development process and feminist's studies have evolved challenging the existing concept of economics and its treatment of women.

Major gaps exist with regard to establishing a substantial link among women's position in the family and society, sexual division of labour and women's participatory process in the public sphere, which needs a better and more articulated explanatory theory. Similarly while regional micro-studies relating to women have been undertaken for various States, studies relating to the State of Mizoram have been almost negligible. This is a serious challenge to researchers dealing specifically with the North-Eastern States, so that new framework for understanding the contribution and participation of women is developed and wider dimension evolved to understand their role in the economy. It is, therefore, our sincere endeavour to take up this study on the vast issue of Gender and Development concentrating this present work mainly on the female work participation and its contribution to socio-economic development. The present study is, therefore, the beginning and only a modest attempt to throw a challenge to future researchers to look into the vast areas of issues involving women and their potential contribution to economic and social development of the North East in general and Mizoram in particular.

## NOTES

1. Mincer, (1962): *Labour Force Participation of Married Women*, Paper in the NBER Volume, Aspects of Labour Economic, Princeton University Press, Houston.
2. Cain, M.T. (1980): *The Economic Activities of Children in a Village in Bangladesh*, Rural Household Studies in Asia, Singapore University Press.
3. *Ibid.*
4. Becker, G. (1964): *Human Capital: A Theoretical and Empirical Analysis with Special Reference to Education*, National Bureau of Economic Research, New York.
5. Mincer, J. and Polacheck, S.W. (1974): 'Family Investments in Human Capital, Earnigs of Women', *Journal of Political Economy*.
6. Krishnan S. (1990): *Women Workers in the Manufacturing Sectors: A District Level Analysis of Selected States 1981*, CSRD, JNU, New Delhi.

7. Chandra, R.C. *et al.* (1964): 'Female Working Force of Rural Punjab', *Manpower Journal,* Vol. II, No. 4.
8. Krishnan, S. (1990): *Women Workers in the Manufacturing Sectors: A District Level Analysis of Selected States 1981,* CSRD, JNU, New Delhi.
9. Whyte, Robert and Pauline Whyte (1982): *The Women of Rural Asia,* West View Press, Boulder, Colorado.
10. Boserup, E. (1970): *Women's Role in Economic Development,* George Allen and Unwin, London.
11. Nath, Kamal (1968): Women in the Working Force in India, *Economic and Political Weekly,* Vol. 3, No. 31.
12. Mitra, Pathak *et al.* (1980): *Status of Women Shifts in Occupational Pattern during 1961-1991,* ICSSR, New Delhi.
13. Kalpagam, U. (1997): *Informal Sector: Emerging Perspective in Development,* Seminar paper, Dec. 22-24, IAMR-IHD, New Delhi.
14. Neetha, N. (1996): *Adverse Sex Ratios and Labour Market Participation of Women: Trends, Patterns and Linkages,* NLI Research Studies,V.V. Giri National Labour Institute.
15. Jayaweera, S. (1997): *Education and Training,* United Nations Commission on the Status of Women, 41st Session, New York.
16. Reddy, C. Ragunatha (1973): *Changing Status of Educational Working Women,* B.R. Publishing Corporation, Delhi.
17. King, E. and M. Hill (1993): *Women's Education in Developing Countries,* John Hopkins Press for the World Bank, Washington D.C.
18. Schultz, T.P. (1993): *Returns to Women's Education.* Chapter 2 in King and Hill (Ed.), John Hopkins Press for World Bank, Washington D.C.
19. Monohar, M.K. (1993): *Socio-economic Status of Indian Women,* AIWC, Delhi, Seema Publishers, New Delhi.
20. Nye, F. Ivan and Hoffman L.M.(1972): *The Employed Mother in America,* Chicago, Rand McNally.
21. Orden, R. and Broadburn, N.M. (1968): 'Working Wives and Marriage Happiness', *The American Journal of Sociology,* Vol. 74.
22. *Indian Journal of Agriculture Economics,* Vol. 40, 1985.
23. Krishna, A.P., (1983): 'Women Technology and Development Process', *Economic and Political Weekly,* Vol. XIV.
24. Chandra, R.C. (1964): 'Female Working Force of Rural Punjab', *Manpower Journal,* Vol. II, No. 4.
25. Sinha, J.N. (1965): 'Rural Employment Planning Dimensions and Constraints', *Economic and Political Weekly,* Vol. VI, No. 6, Annual Number.

26. Sharma, A. and Singh, S. (1993): *Women and Work: Changing Scenario in India*, Indian Society of Labour Economics, B.R. Publications, New Delhi.

27. Bardhan, Kalpana (1985): 'Women's Work, Welfare and Status: Forces of Tradition and Change in India', *Economic and Political Weekly*, September 14th.

28. Banerjee, Nirmala (1985): 'Modernisation and Marginalisation', *Social Scientist*, Vol. 13, No. 10 -11, Oct.-Nov., pp. 48 -69.

29. Gopalan Sarala (1995) : *Women and Employment in India*, Har Anand Publications, New Delhi.

30. Ghosh and Mukhopadhyay (1982): *Sources and Variation in Female Participation Rate: A Decomposition Analysis*, paper for the Seminar on Women's Work and Employment, Indian Social Studies.

31. Acharya (1979): *Transfer of Technology and Women Employment in India*, ICSSR Programme of Women's Studies, Mimeo.

32. Fong, M.S. (1975): *Female Labour Force Participation in a Modernizing Society: Malaya and Singapore*, No. 34. Paper of the East-West Population Institute, 1921-1957.

33. Duvvury Nata (1989): Women in Agriculture: A Review of the Indian Literature, *Economic and Political Weekly*, October 28.

34. Saksena, P. K. (1991) : *Regional Disparities in Female Work Participation Rate in India:*, Discovery Publishing House, New Delhi.

35. Sunderam, K. (1989): Inter-State Variations in Work Force Participation Rate of Women in India: An Analysis, in Limited *Options – Women Workers in Rural India* (ed.), A.V. Jose, ILO.

36. Papola, T.S. and Sharma, A. (1999): *Gender and Employment in India*, Vikas Publishing House, New Delhi.

37. Bell, C.S. (2002): 'Data on Race, Ethnicity and Gender: Caveats for the User', in Martha Fetherolf Loutfi (ed.), *Women Gender and Work*, ILO, Geneva.

38. Becker, G. (1964): *The Economics of Discrimination*, University of Chicago Press, Chicago.

39. Thurow, Lester C. (1975): *Poverty and Discrimination*, D.C. Brooklyn Institution, Washington.

40. Tilak, Jandhyala B. G. (1980): 'Education and Labour Market Discrimination', *Indian Journal of Industrial Relations*, Vol. XVI, 1, July 1980.

41. Banerjee, Nirmala (1985): Modernisation and Marginalisation, *Social Scientist*, Vol. 13, No. 10-11, Oct.-Nov., pp. 48-69.

42. Rehman, Kanta (1995): *Gender Discrimination and Development Process in Labour and Development*, Vol. I, No. I, July-December.

43. Sheikh, A.M. (1999): *Human Resource Development and Management*, S. Chand and Co., New Delhi.

44. Kingdon, Geeta Gandhi (1999): Labour Force Participation, Returns to Education and Sex Discrimination, in *Gender and Employment in India*, T.S. Papola and A.N. Sharma (Ed.), Vikas Publishing House, New Delhi.

45. *Ibid.*

46. Whyte, Robert and Pauline Whyte (1982): *The Women of Rural Asia*, West View Press, Boulder, Colorado.

47. Lalitha Devi, V., (1982): *Status and Employment of Women in India*, New Delhi.

48. Jain, Devaki (1975): *From Dissociation to Rehabilitation*, Allied Publishers, New Delhi.

49. Krishna Raj, M. (1980): *Approaches to Self-Reliance: Some Urban Models*, Popular Prakashan, Bombay.

50. Nayak, Jossie Tellis (1979): *Towards Self-Reliance-Income Generation for Women*, Indian Social Institute, New Delhi.

51. Bagchi, J. (1995): *Indian Women Myth and Reality*, Sangam Books, Hyderabad.

52. Desai, A.R (1994): *Women's Liberation and Politics of Religious Personal Laws in India*, CSSMTP, Mumbai.

53. Dixit, Maitreya (1998): *Women and Achievement - Dynamics of Participation and Partnership*, Krishna Publishers, New Delhi.

54. Mukhopadhya, Swapna (1997): *In the Name of Justice: Women and Law in Society*, Manohar Publishers, New Delhi.

55. Sarkar, Lotika (1995): *Women's Movement and the Legal Process*, Occasional Paper No. 24, CWDS, New Delhi.

# 4

# ECONOMIC PARTICIPATION OF WOMEN

## A Comparative Study of India and Mizoram

### INTRODUCTION

An attempt has been made to analyse the female work participation in Mizoram on the basis of secondary data and also to examine the structure of the labour market on the basis of gender. This could give us a broad idea of the participation of women in Mizoram with respect to the country as a whole in the labour market. For this purpose we have utilized the census data and also reports of various NSS rounds to make this study meaningful.

Women in Mizoram constitute nearly 49 per cent of the total population with almost 43.7 per cent of the total female population working according to 2001 census. Majority of the working women population are engaged in the informal sector and are, therefore, subjected to the discrepancies, which exists in the labour market. Traditional handicrafts, like weaving and bamboo works occupy a prominent place next to agriculture. In Mizoram the impact of the developmental activities on women during the post-Independence period is significant. The role and status of women in Mizoram have undergone notable changes with improvement in literacy and awareness that comes along with development and change in the social and economic life. Yet inequality of status persists in different aspects of economic, social and family life. Inadequate employment opportunities compel women to concentrate in the unorganized sector and they lag behind men in employment in salaried jobs and in sectors, which involve decision-making and exercising power. The worker population ratio in Table 4.1 presents a broad picture of the trend of female work participation *vis-à-vis* male and total work participation rate in India as a whole with urban-rural break up. This is based on Census and NSS reports. From Table 4.1 it may be seen that there has been a decline in the Female Work Participation Rate (henceforth termed as FWPR) with the lowest recorded at 13.9 per cent in the year 1971 Census and marginally rising by 19.8 per cent in 1981, 28.58 per cent in 1991 and 31.6 per cent in 2001 Census. As compared to the FWPR Male Work Participation Rate (henceforth termed as MWPR) has also been declining over the years. Taking one or two figures alone and arriving at definite conclusions would be misleading because of changes in the concept of the definition of workers in the different censuses. However, the changes in the definitional aspect, resulting to the changes in overall aspect indicate the following:

(i) The Female Work Participation Rate in India is far behind that of males for the entire period of our study irrespective of the definition of workers;

(ii) The participation rate for both female and male is increasing over the years; and

(iii) As regards the 1971 and 1981 censuses there was a considerable concern about the undercount of female workers. And hence, 1991 Census was redefined to include 'unpaid workers'. In spite of these changes FWPR according to 1991 census showed only a marginal increase.

**Table 4.1** : Worker Population Ratio in India (By Sex and Residence)

| Sl.No. | Year/NSS round | India | | | Rural India | | | Urban India | | |
|---|---|---|---|---|---|---|---|---|---|---|
| | | P | M | F | P | M | F | P | M | F |
| 1 | **1971 Census** | **34.0** | **52.7** | **13.9** | **36.1** | **53.6** | **15.5** | **29.6** | **48.9** | **07.1** |
| 2 | 1972-78 NSS (27) | 41.3 | 53.5 | 28.2 | 43.5 | 54.5 | 31.8 | 33.1 | 50.1 | 13.4 |
| 3 | 1977-78 NSS (32) | 42.2 | 54.2 | 29.3 | 44.4 | 55.2 | 33.1 | 34.4 | 50.8 | 15.6 |
| 4 | **1981 Census*** | **36.8** | **80.2** | **19.8** | **38.9** | **53.8** | **23.2** | **30.0** | **47.1** | **8.3** |
| 5 | 1982 NSS (38) | 42.2 | 53.8 | 29.6 | 44.6 | 54.7 | 34.0 | 34.3 | 51.2 | 15.1 |
| 6 | 1987-88 NSS (43) | 41.1 | 53.1 | 28.1 | 43.4 | 53.9 | 32.3 | 33.9 | 50.6 | 15.2 |
| 7 | **1991 Census**** | **37.6** | **71.42** | **28.58** | **40.0** | **52.5** | **26.7** | **30.2** | **48.9** | **9.2** |
| 8 | 1990-91 NSS (46) | 40.4 | 54.3 | 25.4 | 42.7 | 55.3 | 29.2 | 33.8 | 51.3 | 14.3 |
| 9 | 1993-94 NSS (50) | 42.0 | 54.5 | 28.6 | 44.4 | 55.3 | 32.8 | 34.7 | 52.0 | 15.4 |
| 10 | 2000-01 NSS (55) | 42.2 | 54.8 | 29.6 | 44.6 | 54.7 | 33.1 | 34.9 | 52.2 | 15.6 |
| 11 | **2001 Census** | **39.1** | **68.4** | **31.6** | **77.1** | **64.2** | **35.8** | **22.9** | **82.5** | **17.5** |

* Excludes Assam ** Excludes Jammu& Kashmir

P: Total Population M: Male F: Female

*Source: Censuses of Population/NSS Rounds, Govt. of India (Various years)*

To overcome the incompatibility of the census reports, a comparison with the NSS reports on work participation rate have been made. While the census reports show that the FWPR registered a rise of 19.8 per cent in 1981 and 22 per cent in the 1991 Census, male participation rate also varied between 1972-73 and 1993-94. FWPR has been more or less stable around 28 per cent in India. This may be perhaps due to inclusion of marginal and subsidiary workers in the estimation of FWPR. As female constitutes a larger proportion of marginal workers, their WPR might have shown an increase, without in anyway implying an improvement in their condition in the labour market.

Before examining the general trend of WPR of India and Mizoram, it is imperative to define the term "worker" irrespective of gender differences. A worker is defined as 'a person who participates in any economically productive activity, which could be either physical or mental in nature'. The work involves not only actual work but also effective supervision and direction of work. Table 4.2 indicates that during the period from 1971 to 1981 the percentage of total workers increased with an annual growth of 3.49 per cent. The WPR of total workers further increased to 37.6 per cent in 1991.The 1971 definition of workers included only such persons whose main activity was economically productive work in the category of workers. As a result, household works and students who have also been participating in economic activity for minor part of their time are excluded from definition of labour force. This definitional change has affected the workers in general but the effect is felt more among the women than men. From Table 4.2 showing the total workers, it further follows that there has been an increase in the proportion of total workers throughout India, Mizoram and in the three Districts of Aizawl, Lunglei and Saiha.

This may be due to an increase in the number of male and female workers in all the areas respectively. Increase

Table 4.2 : Comparison of Work Participation Rate

| | | INDIA | | | MIZORAM | | | AIZAWL DISTRICT | | | LUNGLEI DISTRICT | | | SAIHA DISTRICT | | |
|---|---|---|---|---|---|---|---|---|---|---|---|---|---|---|---|---|
| Year | Det-ail | Num-ber | %WPR | AG% | Number | %WPR | AG% | Number | %WPR | AG% | Num-ber | %WPR | AG% | Num-ber | %WPR | AG% |
| 1971 | TW | 186405113 | 32.91 | – | 149576 | 45.61 | – | – | – | – | – | - | - | - | - | - |
| | FW | 36711290 | 19.69- | – | 65843 | 44.02 | – | – | – | – | – | - | - | - | - | - |
| | MW | 149693823 | 80.30 | – | 83733 | 55.98 | – | – | – | – | – | - | - | - | - | - |
| 1981 | TW | 251455499 | 36.8 | 3.49 | 224364 | 45.44 | 5.0 | 154830 | 45.43 | – | 38160 | 44.11 | - | 29467 | 45.96 | |
| | FW | 49788188 | 19.8 | 3.56 | 97823 | 43.6 | 4.86 | 66936 | 43.23 | – | 15222 | 39.89 | - | 11065 | 37.55 | |
| | MW | 201667311 | 80.2 | 3.47 | 126541 | 56.4 | 5.11 | 87894 | 56.76 | – | 22938 | 60.11 | - | 18402 | 62.45 | |
| 1991 | TW | 314131370 | 37.6 | 2.49 | 337360 | 48.91 | 5.04 | 232487 | 48.59 | 5.02 | 55920 | 50.19 | 4.65 | 50917 | 50.98 | 7.28 |
| | FW | 89767563 | 22.05 | 8.03 | 151205 | 44.82 | 5.46 | 100248 | 43.12 | 4.98 | 24739 | 44.24 | 6.25 | 25963 | 50.99 | 13.5 |
| | MW | 224363807 | 51.08 | 1.13 | 186155 | 55.18 | 4.71 | 132239 | 56.88 | 5.05 | 31181 | 55.76 | 3.59 | 34954 | 49.01 | 8.10 |
| 2001 | TW | 401289511 | 39.1 | 2.77 | 467159 | 52.6 | 3.85 | 162961 | 50.40 | –2.99 | 71791 | 52.30 | 2.84 | 26981 | 44.19 | – |
| | FW | 126802251 | 31.59 | 4.13 | 204151 | 43.70 | 3.50 | 68480 | 42.02 | –3.17 | 30885 | 43.02 | 2.48 | 12060 | 44.70 | – |
| | MW | 274487260 | 68.40 | 2.23 | 263008 | 56.29 | 4.13 | 94481 | 57.98 | –2.86 | 40907 | 56.98 | 3.12 | 14921 | 55.30 | – |

WPR : Work Participation Rate
AG per cent : Annual Growth with reference to last available record
TW : Total Worker, FW : Female Worker, MW : Male Worker
– : Not Available .
*Note* : Saiha District 1981 & 1991are undivided i.e Chhimtuipui district record. 2001 is Saiha District record.
*Source :* Census Reports 1971,1981,1991and 2001 (India & Mizoram), Statistical Hand Book 1981(Chhhimtuipui District).

in female workers during this period may be accounted for by the growth in the literacy rate between the period 1971 to 2001, and this is also indicated with a similar improvement in Mizoram and the three districts under consideration. Besides, greater social awareness among the people to seek monetary value for the services rendered may also be the contributing factors.

A further analysis of the male and female distribution of Work Participation Rate (WPR) shows that the percentage of economically active male population has shown a varying trend. In India the highest WPR recorded in the year 1961 (not shown in the table) and a fall in the year 1971 is perhaps due to changes in the definitional concept of work. The 1961 Census defines a person to be in the labour force if he or she had been engaged in economic activity for a greater part of the past season. On the other hand the 1971 definition is more rigorous in the sense that it involves only those persons whose main activity in the reference year was economically meaningful work.

Analysis of the FWPR trend, has revealed that FWPR for the country as a whole has shown a declining trend throughout the period of our study. FWPR is found to be very poor at 22.05 per cent compared to MWPR of 51.08 per cent in the 1991 Census. Thus, the position of women workers and their participation in productive activity is far below the participation rate of men leaving them vulnerable to exploitation and marginalisation, change of definition of worker notwithstanding.

Female population constitutes a strong force in Mizoram and the proportion of female workers in work participation shows an improving trend like the rest of India. The latest Census (2001) reveals that work participation in Mizoram is much higher than India. The total work participation in Mizoram is 52.6 per cent as against 39.1 per cent in India. The FWPR, according to the 2001 Census is 43.7 per cent as against 31.59 per cent in India for the same period.

MWPR in Mizoram during 2001 census was, however, lower at 56.29 per cent as against 68.4 per cent in India as given in Table 4.2. This indicates a relatively high rate of participation of women workers in Mizoram.

According to 2001 Census, the rise in FWPR could be due to an increase in the rural participation rate in the State of Mizoram (FWPR at 27.29 per cent with a growth rate of 2.96 per cent) as against 22.39 per cent in India. Urban FWPR is 20.25 per cent as against 3.24 per cent in India.[1] The total FWPR of Aizawl District which may be considered as the heart of Mizoram has also shown an improving trend. The percentage of total workers has shown a steady rise, with the district of Aizawl registering the second highest FWPR in 1991 census. The largest concentration of FWPR is undivided Saiha district (50.99 per cent) followed by Lunglei district (44.24 per cent) and Aizawl district (43.12 per cent) during 1991. The annual growth rate of FWPR has also depicted a different rate among the districts varying in between 4.98 per cent for Aizawl, 6.25 per cent (maximum) for Lunglei and 13.5 per cent in Saiha. FWPR in Mizoram declines from 44.82 per cent in 1991 Census to 43.7 per cent in 2001 Census. This decline is also observed in the three districts. In Aizawl district FWPR declined to 42.02 per cent, in Lunglei district it declined to 43.02 per cent and to 44.7 per cent in Saiha district during 2001 as given in Table 4.2. This recent decline in FWPR is perhaps due to definitional change as explained earlier. The overall growth rate of WPR has lagged behind the rising growth of population throughout the period since 1971.

From the overall analysis the following facts emerged:

(i) The FWPR is much lower than MWPR in India and this same trend follows in the state of Mizoram as a whole and its three districts also.

(ii) The overall FWPR is always found to be better in India and Mizoram compared to the three districts, viz., Aizawl, Lunglei and Saiha in Mizoram.

(iii) The annual growth rate of FWPR during 1991 and 2001 censuses is found to be much better in India and Mizoram as a whole than its three districts. Indicating that the position of women in entire three districts needs to be improved in the labour market and also a large section of the women population can be actively involved in various productive activities.

(iv) Another feature, in our analysis, is that although annual growth rate, both for male and female participation, has shown varying trend during the period of our analysis in India, Mizoram and its three districts, there has been a discernible trend towards a decline in the WPR of both males and females in 1991 and 2001 Censuses. The decline in MWPR happens to be more or less uniform and gradual in 1991 but the growth rate of FWPR has been showing an upward move during 1991.Though this may again be mainly attributed to changes in the definitional concept of FWPR in the census, while women's frequent entry and exit as well as re-entry may also distort the real picture of female participation rates.

## OCCUPATIONAL DISTRIBUTION OF WORKERS

A comparison of the occupational distribution of workers reveals that while the number of male workers has been rising in India and Mizoram, the largest concentration of female workers has been in cultivation in Mizoram throughout the reference period. While the annual growth rate of cultivators as a whole declined from 3.30 per cent in 1971 to -1.98 per cent in 2001, the participation of women as agricultural labourers, on the other hand increased throughout the reference period, showing an annual growth rate of 109.4 per cent in 1981 as given in Table 4.3.

**Table 4.3:** Occupational Distribution of Female Workers (Main)

| Year | Total Female Workers | | | Cultivators | | | Agricultural Labourers | | | Household Industry Workers | | | Other workers | | |
|---|---|---|---|---|---|---|---|---|---|---|---|---|---|---|---|
| | Number | % of Total | AG% | Number | % of Total | AG% | Number | % of Total | AG% | Number | % of Total | AG% | Number | % of Total | AG% |
| 1971 | 65843 | 100 | – | 63486 | 96.42 | – | 177 | 0.27 | – | – | – | | 2180 | 3.31 | – |
| 1981 | 97823 | 100 | 4.85 | 84431 | 86.31 | 3.30 | 2113 | 2.16 | 109.38 | 1027 | 1.05 | –5.29 | 10252 | 10.48 | – |
| 1991 | 151205 | 100 | 5.46 | 112043 | 74.10 | 3.27 | 4506 | 2.98 | 11.33 | 1905 | 1.26 | 8.55 | 32751 | 21.66 | 21.95 |
| 2001 | 137022 | 100 | –0.94 | 89861 | 65.6 | –1.98 | 4130 | 3.0 | –0.83 | 1625 | 1.2 | –1.47 | 41406 | 30.2 | 2.64 |
| 1981 | 44806000 | 100 | – | 14826000 | 33.09 | – | 20764000 | 46.34 | – | 204 | 6000 | 4.57 | 7170000 | 16.00 | – |
| 1991 | 62922000 | 100 | 4.04 | 21533000 | 34.22 | 4.52 | 2827000 | 44.93 | 3.61 | 2220000 | 3.53 | 0.85 | 10899000 | 17.32 | 5.2 |
| 2001 | 72857170 | 100 | 1.58 | 25367090 | 32.9 | 1.78 | 22378045 | 38.9 | -2.08 | 4697071 | 6.5 | 11.2 | 20414964 | 21.7 | 8.7 |

Per cent of total : Total Share as a percentage of the Total Female Workers for the year.
AG per cent : Annual Growth Rate with reference to the last available year.
*Source :* Census Reports of Mizoram and India 1971, 1981, 1991 and 2001.

Increasing women participation as agricultural labourers is due to lack of either economic opportunities and lack of alternate choices, which compel women to engage themselves as agricultural labourers. In India female participation as cultivators increased from 33.09 per cent in 1981 to 34.22 per cent in 1991, but later declined to 32.9 per cent in 2001. Female participation as agricultural labourers has been declining from 46.34 per cent in 1981 to 44.93 per cent in 1991 and further declines to 38.9 per cent in 2001 as given in Table 4.3. This decline may be due to the increase in agricultural productivity or a decline in the cultivated area.

The rest of the workers are unevenly spread between household industry workers and other workers. Further it may be added that various promotional government schemes have led to the diversification of economic activities at the all-India level especially in the rural areas causing a decline in the primary sector. But such schemes have failed to take shape in Mizoram. This may be responsible for a continuous increase of female participation as agricultural labourers. Therefore, the dominance of FWPR as agricultural labourers in Mizoram may be due to lack of opportunities in the organized sectors and the absence of employment opportunities in other alternative sectors.

The share of female workers engaged in agriculture and allied activities have declined over the years in India, while at the same time, the participation rate in Mizoram has been increasing over the years. The reasons may be the obsolescence of many non-agricultural occupations dominated by women and the movements of men into mechanized jobs that have replaced these jobs.[2] Mizoram as a whole have registered a fall in the share of women workers in agriculture and allied jobs according to 2001 Census.

But due to slow pace of industrialization in the area, and the rapidly increasing number of job seekers in the State

**Table 4.4.** Details of Jobseekers in India, Mizoram and the three Districts (India's Figures in '000)

| Year | INDIA | | MIZORAM | | AIZAWL DISTRICT | | LUNGLEI DISTRICT | | SAIHA DISTRICT | |
|---|---|---|---|---|---|---|---|---|---|---|
| | Number | AG% | Number | AG% | Number | AG% | Number | AG% | Number | AG% |
| 1971 | 5100 | - | 1046 | - | - | - | - | - | - | - |
| 1980 | 16200 | 13.7 | 8895 | 75.03 | 6394 | - | 1685 | - | 816 | - |
| 1981 | 17838 | 10.11 | 10424 | 1.72 | 7247 | 1.33 | 1902 | 1.29 | 1275 | 5.63 |
| 1985 | 26276 | 10.16 | 14142 | 3.57 | 8526 | 1.76 | 2784 | 4.64 | 2832 | 12.21 |
| 1987 | 32776 | 5.67 | 24307 | 8.19 | 17522 | 0.55 | 2888 | 0.34 | 3897 | 3.76 |
| 1991 | 36300 | 5.67 | - | - | - | - | - | - | - | - |
| 1995 | 36742 | 0.30 | 39690 | - | 29665 | - | 5017 | - | 5208 | - |
| 1997 | 37430 | 1.87 | 45809 | 1.54 | 35062 | 1.82 | 4930 | -0.17 | 5817 | 1.17 |
| 2000 | 41343 | 0.95 | 96233 | 11.00 | 83501 | 13.81 | 7295 | 4.80 | 5437 | -0.65 |
| 2002 | 41172 | -0.04 | 52720 | -4.52 | 33599 | -5.97 | 6999 | -0.41 | 7535 | 3.86 |
| 2004 | 40458 | -0.17 | 31462 | -4.03 | 14153 | -5.79 | 4828 | -3.10 | 8708 | 1.56 |

*Source* : Statistical Handbook of Mizoram 1971-2004.

as seen in the Table 4.4, the situation has not been very conducive for women workers. Consequently with no choice available, women are compelled to seek alternative source of occupation in the agricultural sector. For Mizoram, the increase in the proportion of women workers in the agricultural sector indicates that the option of diversification to non-agricultural employment is increasingly limited for women.

Similarly women's share in other sectors is comparatively smaller than their share in the agricultural sector in Mizoram. This also indicates that the expansion of avenues in paid and secured employment is not shared equally among men and women in the State and its three districts under consideration, which are much more economically backward than the State as a whole. Again the concentration of women in the informal sector occupations is of their choices but rather because there exists no other alternative opportunities of employment available to them.

## RURAL-URBAN DISTRIBUTION OF FWPR : A COMPARISON

Table 4.5 highlights the rural–urban difference in the WPR both for males and females as estimated by the decennial census conducted during 1971-2001. For entire India, the urban female WPR, which is merely 9.2 per cent in the 1991 census, has been considerably lower than the rural FWPR of 26.70 per cent for the same period. The 2001 census also presents the same picture with the urban female WPR of 17.5 per cent, which is lower than the rural female WPR of 31.6 per cent for the same period. This may be due to the difficulty in combining work with household and other duties in urban areas. In contrast work in the family enterprises constitute the main activity in rural areas leading to a rise in WPR.

Moreover, in rural areas unmarried girls, young wives, busy mothers and older women are being forced to seek some kind of employment. In such a condition of survival,

**Table 4.5 :** WPR among Females in both Urban and Rural Areas

*(In percentage)*

| Area | M/F | URBAN | | | | | RURAL | | | | |
|---|---|---|---|---|---|---|---|---|---|---|---|
| | | 1981 | 1991 | | 2001 | | 1981 | 1991 | | 2001 | |
| | | % | % | AG% | % | AG% | % | % | AG% | % | AG% |
| India | F | 08.3 | 9.20 | 1.08 | 17.5 | 9.02 | 23.2 | 26.70 | 1.51 | 31.6 | 1.84 |
| | M | 47.1 | 48.90 | 0.38 | 82.5 | 6.87 | 53.8 | 52.50 | -0.24 | 68.4 | 3.03 |
| Mizoram | F | 5.25 | 12.91 | 14.59 | 20.25 | 5.69 | 27.38 | 21.05 | -2.42 | 27.29 | 2.96 |
| | M | 10.73 | 21.80 | 10.32 | 27.04 | 2.4 | 37.4 | 27.78 | -2.57 | 30.24 | 0.89 |
| Aizawl | F | 6.38 | 15.75 | 14.69 | 28.57 | 8.14 | 26.66 | 17.34 | -3.5 | 14.55 | -1.6 |
| Lunglei | F | 2.92 | 9.5 | 22.53 | 15.27 | 6.07 | 26.05 | 23.99 | -0.8 | 31.65 | 3.19 |
| Saiha | F | 2.35 | 2.95 | 2.55 | 6.71 | 12.75 | 32.86 | 35.68 | 0.86 | 33.74 | -0.5 |

AG % : Annual Growth Rate with reference to last available record.

*Source : Census of India and Mizoram, 1981, 1991 and 2001.*

Statistical Handbook of Mizoram, 1981, 1991 and 2001.

work opportunities are uppermost in the minds of women which enable them to detach themselves from the social stigma attached to work in the field. As a result FWPR in the rural areas is much higher than the participation rate in the urban areas of India, Mizoram and the three districts. Comparatively WPR in rural India is higher than the MWPR of the urban areas, while the reversed trend is observed in Mizoram. MWPR has shown either a decline or maintained the same growth after 1981 census whereas FWPR, which showed a decline in the earlier census, has shown a considerable increase in the subsequent censuses. However, in all cases, FWPR always remain much below MWPR in both urban and rural areas.

In recent years men have increasingly moved to the urban areas in search of job opportunities, mainly due to low productive manual work of cultivation in rural areas. These jobs are left to be done by their womenfolk leading to a rise in rural FWPR. This is one of the crucial factors responsible for feminization of agriculture. This, in no way, means that the position of rural women workers has improved, since it is only due to a fall in the relative returns to agricultural labour. This is evident from the fact that the share of agricultural and allied activities to GDP has declined from 52 per cent in 1951 to 29 per cent in 1991, while the share of workforce has only slightly declined from 73 per cent to 65 per cent during the corresponding period. This has resulted in a fall in marginal productivity of agricultural labourers and in wage rate. As a result male workers, who had, at one time flocked to this sector, have started moving out of this sector leaving it to their female counterparts.

This study also revealed that there was a rapid expansion in public activities particularly in the health and rural development activities during the eighties. It is interesting to note that women happens to be the chief beneficiaries of these activities, which might also be another factor responsible for rising the level of FWPR in rural areas. Post reform period has also witnessed diversion of land from food crops to cultivation like floriculture and horticulture, which employ a growing number of female workers. This trend may, therefore, be another reason leading to a rise in FWPR in the rural sector. Another notable feature that have been observed is that :

(i) MWPR has been maintaining the near zero or even slightly negative growth rate in both urban and rural areas in 1991 and 2001 Censuses.

(ii) An improvement of FWPR in the urban sector from 8.3 per cent to 9.2 per cent and 23.2 per cent to 26.7 per cent in rural areas between 1981 and 1991 and to 17.5 per cent in urban sector and to 31.6 per cent in rural areas in 2001 could also mean a better coverage of women workers in the census reports.

In Mizoram and its three districts, the growth rate of FWPR is found to be increasing at a better pace in the rural area than in the urban area during 1981 and 2001 (Table 4.5). This trend is also observed in India. This implies that women are engaged in agriculture and allied activities, which are subject to discriminatory wages. The factor operating at the all India level leading to this trend of FWPR in the labour market may also be operative in this region. It may be noted further that the handloom and sericulture, which were predominantly household activities are now becoming highly commercialized. This has necessitated employment of larger number of labourers in these activities at a lower wage rate. For women the dependency poses additional problem because this sector of the economy is largely characterized by irregularities of jobs, seasonal nature of work with no fixed hours of work. In this case, burden of women is immense as work in this sector is often combined with full time household work. In the urban sector male participation has recorded a slight increase during the two-census period of 1981 and 1991 and increase further in 2001 Census, implying that there has been a gradual shifting of male workers from the rural to urban sectors leaving the female workers to survive under conditions of discriminatory wages. The economy of Mizoram being primarily agrarian, majority of the women workforce still concentrate in agriculture and allied activities. Paddy being the principal crop requires and employs more women for sowing, transplanting and harvesting.

Data relating to urbanization and structure of occupation in urban areas reflects the slow growth of economic development in the State. Urban population according to 2001 Census comprises 49.6 per cent of the population as against the all India average of 27.8 per cent. In the absence of urban development, absorption of labour force from the rural sector is very low. This perhaps could explain the heavy concentration of workers in the rural sector and female labour forces lacking in educational skill and knowledge with no hope for horizontal mobility often have to fend for themselves as marginal workers with low paid structure. One reason for the high concentration of marginal workers in the three districts may also be due to migration of menfolk to work outside their villages and districts.

## EMPLOYMENT IN THE ORGANISED SECTOR

Organised sector is the one which provides regular wages, assured jobs, where the terms and conditions of jobs are regulated strictly within the framework of the labour laws and are enacted to regulate the working hours, working conditions, wages and benefits of the workers. Any tendency of exploitation of the employees by the employers is thus prevented.

A look at the data of organized sector in Table 4.6 for the period 2000 to 2003 in India reveals that the proportion of male employment in the public sector and private sector is much higher than the female employment in both the sectors throughout the period.

Table 4.6 shows that comparatively public sector has been able to provide a larger quantum of employment both

**Table 4.6 :** Employments in the Organised Sector *(India's Figure In Lakh Persons)*

| | Reference period | MIZORAM | | | | INDIA | | | |
|---|---|---|---|---|---|---|---|---|---|
| | | 2000 | 2001 | 2002 | 2003 | 2000 | 2001 | 2002 | 2003 |
| **Public Sector** | Male | 486 | 485 | 481 | 478 | 164.57 | 162.79 | 158.86 | 156.75 |
| | Male AG% | – | –0.2 | -0.01 | –0.6 | – | –1.08 | –2.4 | –1.33 |
| | Female | 249 | 244 | 243 | 240 | 28.57 | 28.59 | 28.87 | 29.05 |
| | Female AG% | – | –2.0 | –0.4 | –1.23 | – | 0.07 | 0.98 | 0.62 |
| | Total | 735 | 729 | 724 | 718 | 193.14 | 191.38 | 187.73 | 185.80 |
| | Total AG% | – | –0.8 | –0.7 | –0.8 | – | -0.91 | –1.91 | –1.03 |
| **Private Sector** | Male | – | – | – | – | 65.80 | 65.62 | 63.83 | 63.57 |
| | Male AG% | – | – | – | – | – | -0.27 | –2.73 | –0.40 |
| | Female | – | – | – | – | 20.66 | 20.90 | 20.49 | 20.64 |
| | Female AG% | – | – | – | – | – | 1.16 | –1.97 | 0.73 |
| | Total | – | – | – | – | 86.46 | 86.52 | 84.32 | 84.21 |
| | Total AG% | – | – | – | – | – | 0.07 | –2.54 | –0.13 |
| **Public & Private Sector** | Male | – | – | – | – | 230.27 | 228.40 | 222.71 | 220.32 |
| | Male AG% | – | – | – | – | – | -0.81 | –2.5 | –1.07 |
| | Female | – | – | – | – | 49.23 | 49.49 | 49.35 | 49.68 |
| | FemaleAG% | – | – | – | – | – | 0.53 | –0.28 | 0.67 |
| | Total | – | – | – | – | 279.60 | 277.89 | 272.06 | 270.00 |
| | AG% | – | – | – | – | – | -0.61 | –2.10 | –0.76 |

*Source:* Office Records and Document, Govt. of Mizoram.

to men and women in comparison to the private sector. In recent years the rate of growth of female employment in private sector is increasing at a higher rate than in the public sector. The growth is, however, found to be rather minimal particularly in public sector which has registered a negative growth for male and female registering a near zero growth. The steady rise in female employment in both the sectors, although encouraging, remain much lower than the rise in male employment in both the sectors. The reason for the overall low participation of women may be hidden in the complexity of factors. But in situations and societal conditions where both male and female unemployment and job-seekers are high, it is the women who are discriminated and pushed to lower rung of the occupational ladder and thus not given a fair chance in the job market. Secondly, tradition and gender biasness have kept many areas out of bounds from women. Regarding the recent increase in women's employment, the Employment Market Information Programme, which collects employment statistics for the organized sectors, has revealed that though employment for women has increased in the organized sector. It takes place mostly in what is possibly the most backward and low paying segments of organized industry.

While analyzing manufacturing sectors in the public sectors, it has been found that this sector had been growing during the nineties without commensurate growth in employment. Studies have shown that employment elasticity of the sector declined from about 1.2 in the 1970s to 0.23 during the period 1988-1994.[3] Uncertainty of work in the manufacturing sector was not only confined to women alone, but casual work was also on the increase for men. But the gap between male and female earnings in casual work nevertheless remained large and this could be attributed to the differences in the nature of their job between the two sexes.[4]

Between 2000 and 2003, male employment in the public sector declined and their numbers fell in almost all industrial categories including manufacturing sector. Considering the overall situation in India, there has been a gradual decline in the share of male and female employment in the secondary sector and particularly in the manufacturing sector. This decline has been severe for urban females where the percentage of women workers engaged in manufacturing sector in the urban areas declined sharply in the late 1980s and early 1990s.

The NSS study (50th Round, 1993-94) similarly point out that female employment is gradually shifting towards tertiary sector with no indication of women shifting towards more productive sectors.[5]

Female employment in the private sector has more or less maintained a steady growth as compared to the public sector. This is perhaps due to the fact that for the private sector; women are assets where the employers are 'used to attributing little value to female labour and women are willing to work for pittance wages at irregular hours in abject working conditions. Few women hope to climb the promotional ladder and remain at the lower rung of the working class'. This has resulted in an upsurge in women's employment in the private sector though not to their advantage.

In Mizoram, there is no organized private sector; therefore, Table 4.6 shows employment in the public sector alone. The number of female employed in the organized public sector is far below the total number of employment among the males. The annual growth rate registered a negative growth for both male and female during the period 2000 to 2003. The reason for the negative growth in the public sector in Mizoram is that the State Government signed a Memorandum of Understanding (MoU) with the Central Government not to create any additional employment vacancies and not to give employment to others when any of their employees passed away or retired. Moreover these public sector undertakings, of the State Government are running at a loss and with no profit, it is not possible for these sectors to create additional employment. There is a need to privatize these public sector undertakings of the Government so as to make them a profit making bodies.

A comparison with the all India situation shows that the proportion of female employment in the organized sector, both in India as well as in Mizoram is far below that of male employment, which signifies that in spite of growing literacy, employment of women in the organized sector is still negligible. While in India almost 29 lakh women were employed in the organized sector in 2000, only 249 females were employed in Mizoram for the same year. Poor representation of females in the organized sector speaks about the exploitation of women. It is clear in the overall scenario; the total number of males employed in the organized sector far exceeds that of female participation. This reveals deterioration in the status of workers, particularly women in the Indian labour force, which may be due to various demographic pressures, slow growth and poor labour absorption in the organized sectors. In India, the share of female employment in the public sector is much higher with 29.05 lakh females as against only 20.64 lakh females in the private sector for the period 2003. Whereas in Mizoram, employment share of females in the public sector are only 240 in 2003. Male workers share in the public sector is 156.75 lakhs in India and 478 in Mizoram for the period 2003. Therefore, the question that emerges is why the percentage of women to total employees is more adverse in the public sector in Mizoram. The answers are hidden behind a complex matrix of social and cultural factors and a few explanations may be stated as follows:

(a) In the absence of sufficient development and expansion of public sector, which assures a stable employment, overall employment opportunity for both males and females in this sector, has become restricted.

(b) Prevalent patriarchy reinforces the belief that women are basically supplementary earners and, therefore, in a job-scarce economy societal attitudes justify elbowing women out of the job queues.

(c) Gender bias and tradition have kept many large sectors out of bounds for women areas such as electricity generation and transmission, petroleum, gas and construction.

On the other hand, women are mostly considered assets in the private sector, where prescribed norms do not govern the labour market and hence women workers could be made to fluctuate according to the whims and fancies of their employers. As Kalpana Bardhan[6] points out, "the ideology of patriarchy makes the exclusion from higher wages, regular jobs and trade unions acceptable to the rising number of women grinding away at the lowest wages, nursing only the expectation of potential access for husband or son into the privileged workforce of the organized sector."

## EMPLOYMENT IN THE UNORGANISED SECTOR

The unorganized workers include people working in agriculture and agriculture related work, forest workers, usher folks, construction labourers, workers employed in small scale/ancillary centre in the informal sector of industry, domestic workers, anganwadi workers, casual labourers, home-bored workers and self-employed workers.

The number of workers in the unorganized sector increases rapidly and steadily for various reasons. The firm and enterprises in the highly competitive market try to reduce costs. Certain aspects of the labour process are entrusted to cheap labour. The agricultural labour is too weak in the context of the rising growth of small enterprises like small retail shops, hotels and restaurants and repair shops. Workers in the unorganized sector are unprotected by law and they are the most vulnerable sections of the society with low bargaining power.[7]

The unorganized sector is thus used here to mean the informal, traditional and unregulated sector. This sector employs a large proportion of workers both men and women in India. According to an estimate of the National Commission on Self-Employment of Women, 92 per cent of the total female workforce operates in the unorganized sector. Wages in this sector tend to be extremely low leading to high levels of poverty that affects the overall health of a woman and children in terms of calorie intake, health-care and education which, in turn, reflected the low level of human development.

It may be noted here that the task of carrying out periodic survey on the unorganized sector activities in the interim period has been entrusted with the National Sample Survey Organisation.

Due to lack of similar comparable data for Mizoram and the three districts, viz., Aizawl, Lunglei and Saiha, a comparative study has not been possible. However, the overall picture of India emerges from Table 4.7. This table projects only a rough estimate of the size of female employment in the unorganized sector for rural and urban areas.

**Table 4.7:** Estimated Female Employment in the Unorganised Sector by Residence

| Sl. No. | Residence | 1972-73 | 1977-78 | 1983 | 1987-88 |
|---|---|---|---|---|---|
| 1 | Urban | 7.76 | 11.05 | 12.71 | 15.11 |
| 2 | Rural | 66.99 | 75.81 | 80.71 | 85.79 |
| 3 | Total | 74.75 | 86.86 | 93.42 | 100.90 |

*Sources* : Estimated from Reports on Quinquennial Surveys on Employment and Unemployment, NSSO, Various Issues; Directorate General of Employment and Training (DGET) data reported in manpower profiles of India, IAMR.

The incidence of women in unorganized sector or informal sector is much higher for both rural and urban location. This may be explained in general by the reproductive role and responsibilities of women, which determine their supply in the labour market. According to Table 4.7, the largest concentration of unorganised female workers is in rural area (85.79 million). In all the cases of urban, rural and overall picture, the growth rate of FWPR in the unorganised sector has the same trend with high growth rate during 1977-78 followed by a reduced rate in 1983 and again a rising trend in 1987-88. However, the trend displays a rising growth in unorganised female workers in the rural areas. Study on the unorganized manufacturing by Mukhopadhyay[8] provides information on the number of enterprises and gender disaggregated in own account and non-directory establishment at the digit-level for India. It has been observed that employment is highest in own account enterprises, which are run primarily with family labour and presumably at low earnings as well as low productivity. In the rural areas own account enterprises work out to be 43.61 per cent as against 37.11 per cent in the urban area whereas non-directory enterprises in the rural area stand out to be 12.9 per cent as against 5.41 per cent in the urban area.

From the above figures it is evident that female employment is comparatively much higher in the smallest units of production, which provide low earnings as well as low economic stability in India.

Self-employment accounts for a substantial proportion of women workers in Mizoram. The problem lies in the fact that majority of these workers are unpaid workers with no authority to exercise their decisions in the family enterprises and this kind of workers constitute for nearly half the women engaged in traditional family based occupations.

The concentration of a good number of females in agriculture and allied activities in Mizoram is a reflection of the growing poverty, which pushes a growing number of women into agricultural sector. Despite their increasing prominence in the agricultural labour force, rural women are not absorbed in many of the jobs outside agriculture that are developing in the rural areas.

The percentage of females working as agricultural labourers has increased in Mizoram during 1991 and 2001 census (Table 4.3). This again may be due to better coverage in the latest census or it may also be due to greater participation of women in supplementing the household income. In recent years there has been an increase in the relative number of women agricultural labourers as opposed to cultivators. This change in their status, however, does not assign decision-making power to the females on the family plots. Such powers are vested within the men folk. Men are gradually moving out to towns looking for greener pastures leaving the low productivity manual work to the women folk in addition to non-manual work. Higher incidence of female workers as agricultural labourers is available in Mizoram and in the Aizawl, Lunglei and Saiha districts due to intensive cultivation of commercial crops such as rice and other cash crops grown under favourable climatic endowments. Females constitute a very marginal proportion of workers in all the other sectors of the unorganized sector of the country and the State of Mizoram.

This implies that in the absence of productive employment in the organized sector of the economy, females are marginalised and pushed into the unorganized sector. And because women in the unorganized sector are less skilled and less educated they are marginally employed drawing lower wages.

Women also supply a major portion of labour in the production of cash crops. But there is discrimination against women here also. While women are usually responsible for the strenuous job of weeding and transplanting, men control the production of commercial crops and derive profits by selling such crops. With an increase in the density of population land become divided and again subdivided leaving to fragmentation of land. So women are required to walk longer and longer distances, as they have to move from one field to another.

Due to resource constraints and risk of financial investments women in female-headed households are forced to remain engaged in traditional modes of economic activity. As a result, their productivity stagnates while that of men continues to rise. Since women are generally restricted to low-productivity informal sector employment and have to bear higher dependency burdens, they invariably remain poor and malnourished thereby depriving them a chance to obtain formal education, health-care and sanitation. In fact, the economic welfare of women and children within poor families depends to a considerable extent on the economic status of women. This means that just as per capita income is also an inadequate measure of absolute poverty; household income is a poor measure of individual welfare. The reason may be sought in the vast unequal distribution of income within the family.

Many women run small business, called micro enterprises, which require very little initial capital and often involve the marketing of food articles and handicrafts produced under domestic (rather than factory) system. No doubt women's limited access to capital leads to higher rates of return on their tiny investments. But the unbelievably low capital-ratios confine women to low productivity undertakings.

It is obvious that the concept of workers has been changing in successive censuses and some even do not have a comparable data of women and their exact contributions to economic work. There is an exclusion of a whole range of activities performed by women, the unpaid economic activities, their economic contribution in work through domestic sectors; their long hours of household work remaining unaccounted. The contribution of women must be accounted for and treated as essential factors in the economic growth of the country.

MARGINAL WORKERS AND WORK PARTICIPATION RATE

The concept of marginal workers was introduced in the 1981 census. A marginal worker consists of people who report for work for some time during a year but not long enough to qualify them as main workers.

The detail is indicated in Table 4.8. Table 4.8 depicts the picture for female and male marginal workers for 1991 and 2001 Censuses. A comparative scenario based on this Census has been drawn for India and Mizoram for marginal workers as a percentage to the respective total workers. In all the cases it is evident that women are most marginalized section of the society with highest concentration in all the rural areas in 2001, ranging from 14.1 per cent in India, 16.9 per cent in Mizoram, 18.5 per cent in Aizawl, 11.7 per cent in Lunglei and 17.6 per cent in Saiha. However, in urban areas, female marginal workers hover around 9 per cent to 14 per cent in 2001. This is a clear indication of the existence of the ideology of patriarchy, the presence of which is being experienced constantly into the material base of capitalist relation and which has been reinforced by the type of development in the Indian countryside.[9]

Feminist studies have, therefore, repeatedly pointed out that capitalist penetration has led to the pauperization and has been affected the most.[10]

Again in the overall scenario of 2001 Census, female marginal workers are found to outnumber their male counterparts. Comparatively percentage of male workers is less than 9 per cent in case of urban areas and 1.3 per cent to 7.8 per cent in case of rural area. Mizoram registered the highest percentage of marginal male workers of 7.8 per cent, which is also the rate of India during the same period.

In 1991 census, the female marginal workers outnumber

**Table 4.8** : Percentages of Marginal Workers to Total Workers

| Area | Year | Urban | | | Rural | | | Overall | | |
|---|---|---|---|---|---|---|---|---|---|---|
| | | Male | Female | Total | Male | Female | Total | Male | Female | Total |
| India | 1991 | 0.72 | 11.35 | 2.24 | 1.37 | 30.8 | 10.7 | 1.21 | 28.4 | 8.98 |
| | 2001 | 3.4 | 2.5 | 3.0 | 7.8 | 14.1 | 10.9 | 6.6 | 11.0 | 8.7 |
| Mizoram | 1991 | 2.47 | 5.25 | 7.71 | 2.09 | 4.14 | 6.23 | 1.59 | 9.38 | 13.94 |
| | 2001 | 8.6 | 14.4 | 11.4 | 7.8 | 16.9 | 12.2 | 6.6 | 15.6 | 11.8 |
| Aizawl District | 1991 | 2.89 | 5.98 | 8.87 | 1.92 | 3.95 | 5.87 | 4.51 | 10.03 | 7.17 |
| | 2001 | 8.5 | 13.0 | 10.7 | 2.52 | 18.5 | 14.2 | 8.9 | 14.3 | 11.6 |
| Lunglei District | 1991 | 2.66 | 6.19 | 8.86 | 2.43 | 4.01 | 6.45 | 4.89 | 10.7 | 7.68 |
| | 2001 | 5.8 | 9.6 | 7.6 | 5.1 | 11.7 | 8.2 | 5.4 | 10.8 | 8.0 |
| Saiha District | 1991 | – | – | – | 2.37 | 4.99 | 7.36 | 2.58 | 5.63 | 8.21 |
| | 2001 | – | – | – | 7.3 | 17.6 | 12.3 | 6.4 | 14.2 | 10.2 |

*Source:* 1. Census of India and Mizoram, 1991 and 2001,
2. Statistical Handbook of Mizoram, 1991 and 2001.

their male counterparts. The percentage of male workers is less than 2.8 per cent in case of urban areas and from 1.3 per cent to 2.4 per cent in rural areas. Aizawl has the highest concentration of male marginal workers with 2.9 per cent.

In 2001, the incidence of female marginal workers is found to be most severe in rural areas of Aizawl. Lack of industrialization and inadequate expansion of employment opportunities has driven the workforce to eke out a living in the rural sector of the economy.

Though FWPR has increased both in the rural and urban areas of India, the percentage of increase in the female marginal workers is greater than the simultaneous increase in male marginal workers. This similar trend is also observed throughout the State of Mizoram and in the three districts of Aizawl, Lunglei and Saiha, with the largest concentration located in Aizawl district (18.5 per cent) according to 2001 Census. In the overall analysis, marginal female workers constitute a much larger proportion of the total female workers, while the proportion for male marginal workers to the total male workers is much less in comparison.

These figures demonstrate the severity of marginalisation among female than male. This is a clear indication of discrimination, which is ingrained within the employment system. Such segregation brings about earning differentials, which is justified by the existence of marked differences in human capital endowment between males and females. Much of the discrimination had become institutionalized as a result of persistent marginalisation.

This may indicate the following :

1. There is an exclusion of women from main productive employment and hence a decline in the share of wages for women;
2. There is concentration of women in sectors, which are considered to be low paid, or underpaid sectors;

3. A categorization of women in certain types of jobs, which are low in the occupational hierarchy and are low paying, which are ordinarily referred to as feminisation in employment; and
4. Economic inequality which is reflected in wage differentials may in the long-run affect the women's economic position and decision-making capabilities of an individual.

### WORK PARTICIPATION AND POPULATION

A study for the period of 1971 to 2001 reveals that overall population has increased throughout the period, with India maintaining lead followed by Mizoram and its districts. This is indicated in Table 4.9.

The annual growth rate of population increase for India was 2.5 per cent in 1971, which increased to 2.35 per cent in 1981 and further to 2.13 per cent in 1991 to 2001.

The growth rate of total WPR for the same period as indicated in Table 4.2 shows a marginally high rate at 3.49 per cent in 1971 to 1981 and this rate fell to 2.49 per cent during 1981 to 1991 followed by another marginal gain of 2.77 per cent during 1991 to 2001.

While maintaining a higher annual growth rate of population of 4.9 per cent from 1971 to 1981 Mizoram has reversed their rate to 2.88 per cent thereby rapidly catching up the all India average of 2.13 per cent by 2001. However, for Lunglei district this growth rate is found to be little higher during 2001 at 7.5 per cent. In Aizawl district the annual growth rate from 1981 to 1991 is 4.04 per cent, which is higher than the all India growth rate of 2.35 per cent in 1991.

As revealed in Table 4.9, the 1981 and 1991 Censuses data of Saiha district represent the undivided figure of Chhimtuipui district. Only 2001 Census represent record of the present Saiha district. Between 1981 and 1991 Saiha

**Table 4.9 : Population Analysis**

| Area | Type | 1971 | | 1981 | | | 1991 | | | 2001 | | |
|---|---|---|---|---|---|---|---|---|---|---|---|---|
| | | TP | % of TP | TP | % of TP | AG% | TP | % of TP | AG% | TP | % of TP | AG% |
| India | Total | 548159652 | 100 | 685185000 | 100 | 2.5 | 846302688 | 100 | 2.35 | 1026443540 | 100 | 2.13 |
| | Male | 284049350 | 51.82 | 354398000 | 51.72 | 2.48 | 439230458 | 51.90 | 2.39 | 531061138 | 51.74 | 2.09 |
| | Female | 264110302 | 48.18 | 330787000 | 48.57 | 2.52 | 407072230 | 48.10 | 2.31 | 495382402 | 48.26 | 2.17 |
| Mizoram | Total | 332390 | 100 | 493757 | 100 | 4.85 | 689756 | 100 | 3.97 | 888573 | 100 | 2.88 |
| | Male | 170824 | 52.84 | 257239 | 52.10 | 5.06 | 358978 | 52.04 | 3.96 | 459109 | 51.67 | 2.79 |
| | Female | 161566 | 49.98 | 236518 | 47.90 | 6.50 | 330778 | 47.96 | 3.99 | 429464 | 48.33 | 2.98 |
| Aizawl District | Total | – | – | 340826 | 100 | – | 478465 | 100 | 4.04 | 562855 | 100 | 1.76 |
| | Male | – | – | 176242 | 51.71 | – | 248343 | 51.90 | 4.09 | 287653 | 51.11 | 1.58 |
| | Female | – | – | 164584 | 48.29 | 230122 | 48.09 | 3.98 | 275202 | 48.89 | 1.96 | – |
| Lunglei District | Total | – | – | 86511 | 100 | – | 111415 | 100 | 2.88 | 195179 | 100 | 7.52 |
| | Male | – | – | 45998 | 53.17 | – | 58331 | 52.35 | 2.68 | 101521 | 52.01 | 7.40 |
| | Female | – | – | 40513 | 46.82 | – | 53084 | 47.65 | 3.10 | 93658 | 47.99 | 7.64 |
| Saiha district | Total | – | – | 66420 | 100 | – | 99876 | 100 | 5.04 | 61056 | 100 | – |
| | Male | – | – | 34999 | 52.69 | – | 52304 | 52.37 | 4.94 | 31241 | 51.17 | – |
| | Female | – | – | 31421 | 47.30 | – | 47572 | 47.63 | 5.14 | 29841 | 48.87 | – |

TP: Total Population, AG per cent: Annual Growth with reference to last available record.
-Not Available
*Note:* Saiha district 1981&1991 are undivided (i.e.Chhimtuipui) record, 2001 is Saiha District record.
*Source:* Census of India and Mizoram (Various years).

district have an annual growth rate of 5.04 per cent, which is the highest in the reference period.

The yearly growth rate of the total population and WPR for Mizoram from 1971 to 2001 is also indicated in Table 4.9. While the growth of population has been 2.88 per cent, the corresponding growth of WPR has been 3.85 per cent. In Aizawl district, growth of population is 1.76 per cent and WPR has been –2.99 per cent during the same period. In Lunglei district population growth has been 7.5 per cent and WPR has been 2.84 per cent in the same period, i.e. 1971 to 2001. The same is not shown for Saiha district because the district was undivided during 1981 to 1991 as stated above. This clearly shows that overall growth rate in WPR have never kept pace with the overall growth rate of population.

Similarly, the growth rate of work participation of females shows a varying trend while growth rate of population was steady. However, it may be noted that a significant improvement took place in FWPR over the MWPR between 1971 to 2001 Censuses.

While this may present a very optimistic picture, however, the participation has remained below the MWPR and total WPR. Further women are always discriminated when the question of providing stable and assured jobs arises.

The sudden decline in the rate of growth of MWPR during 1991 with respect to 1971 is perhaps due to change in definitional aspect in census. The sudden spurt in the rate of growth of FWPR during 1991 with respect to 1971 could also be due to definitional change. However, from 1971 to 2001 the growth rate of FWPR and female population for India were 4.13 per cent and 2.17 per cent respectively. For the same period Mizoram have shown a growth rate of FWPR of 3.5 per cent as against the population growth rate of 2.98 per cent. In Aizawl district the growth rate of FWPR and female population were –

3.17 per cent during 1991 to 2001 and 1.96 per cent during 1971 to 1991. In Lunglei district FWPR growth rate is 2.48 per cent and female population growth rate is 7.6 per cent respectively.

In Mizoram expansion of service and other employment creating sectors has not been commensurate with the overall increase in population. Sex ratio and literacy rate, which works out to be fairly high, is indicative of growing increase in social awareness among the people. However, non-absorption of the growing number of job seekers has failed to harness the full potentiality of women as an important economic category of population.

The sex ratio in India has always been found to be adverse to women and has been declining over the decades with slight improvement during 1981 Census. However, in Mizoram the sex ratio has been increasing throughout the period, from 925 in 1991 Census to 935 in 2001 Census. The steady rise in sex ratio and literacy rate in Mizoram and the three districts under consideration could be an indicator of the increase in social awareness amongst the people. This, coupled with an improvement in the FWPR could harness the full potentiality of women as an important economic category of population.

It is a fact that wide discrepancy exists in work participation rate among females. But it is also true that millions of women work within the home without any remuneration to take care of the home and the household. But such household workers do not clearly figure in either the census or official statistics and thus presents a distorted picture of the real FWPR. This again highlights the poor and exploitative representation of female workers in the overall scenario.

It is thus clear that with the overall increase in population. FWPR either in Mizoram or India is much lower *vis-à-vis* MWPR. With the increase in population, combined with a poor representation in the total workforce, the unemployment in the female population is found to be alarming. The dependency ratio, that is, proportion of non-workers to total population is high and unemployment both in a disguised form is equally rampant in the districts. The increasing working population is again heavily concentrated in rural areas and not in the urban sectors. This shows that there exists symptoms of reliance and subsistence economy where marginalisation of women workforce is high and situation of being underpaid; unrecognized and unremunerative jobs are common. Their economic contribution in work through domestic sectors; their long hours of household work remain unaccounted. The contribution of women must be accounted for and treated as essential factors in the economic growth of a country.

INCIDENCE OF UNEMPLOYMENT

Table 4.4 gives the number of job seekers registered with the employment exchanges. Since comparable data on Mizoram with India does not exist and the magnitude of unemployment in Mizoram is precisely not known, we can have an idea about the trend and dimension of the problem from the number of job seekers registered with the employment exchanges.

Table 4.4 reveals that the number of job seekers registered with employment exchanges, which, during 1980 was only 16,200 thousand in India, 8,895 in Mizoram, 6,394 in Aizawl district, 1,685 in Lunglei district and 816 in Saiha district. The number increased sharply during 1994 to 36,742 thousand in India, 39,690 in Mizoram, 29,665 in Aizawl district, 5,017 in Lunglei and 5,208 in Saiha district. Since 2002 there has been a negative annual growth rate in India and Mizoram, the live register in employment exchanges decreased in India from 4,11,72,000 in 2002 to 4,04,58,000 in 2004, in Mizoram live registered decline from 52,720 to 31,462 during the same period. Though the annual growth of job seekers, which may be taken as indicative of growth rate of unemployment, has registered a fall for India, it has slightly increased in Mizoram. This could be due to lack of employment opportunities in Mizoram in the private sector, which could have accommodated a large number of unemployed youths in the rest of the country in the unorganized sector.

In the year 2000-2001 the number of live register in employment exchanges in Mizoram was 96,233 which sharply declined to 52,720 in 2002 and further to 31,462 in 2004. If there is a positive relation between job seekers and employment growth this should reflect a very high growth rate of employment in Mizoram. But in reality employment growth rate is low. This indicated that those who registered themselves in the employment exchanges failed to renew their registration because they lost confidence in the employment exchanges, since almost all the vacant posts in the State are advertised and filled up, and jobs might have been created and absorbed without the knowledge of the employment exchanges. Therefore, educated persons do not renew their registration nor feel the need to register them, thereby leading to a fall in the numbers in the live registered. The other reason for the decline in the number of live registered in employment exchanges in Mizoram could also be due to the expansion of job opportunities in areas such as information technology, fashion technology, Institute of Tourism and Fashion Technology (ITFT), Department of Electronics Accreditation and Computer Centre (DOEACC) etc. where there is no requirement of registration in employment exchanges.

In Saiha district the number of job seekers has been continuously increasing during the period 1980 to 2004 except for the year 2000 where the number of live registered falls to 5,437 from 5,817. In Lunglei district also the number of job seekers increased from 1,685 in 1980 to 5,017 in 1996 and increases further to 7,295 in 2000, but declined to 4,828 in 2004 due to the same factors sited above for Mizoram as a whole. In Aizawl district the number of live register increased gradually from 6,394 in 1980 to 84,501 in 2000 but later declined sharply to 14,253 in 2004. This is also due to the same reasons that caused a decline in the number of job seekers registered for the State as a whole.

A conclusion may be drawn here that the total number of job seekers declined but this is not reflected in the employment sector. This signifies that there still exists a large stock of usable manpower both in the State and in the three districts, which are not being exploited. The employment statistics reveal only the trend and not the totality of unemployment as all unemployed do not register themselves with the employment exchanges which are mostly located in the urban areas like cities and towns.

Though category-wise detailed comparable data are not available, there exists a huge extent of under-employment or disguised unemployment in the rural areas of which the sizeable proportion are woman workers. The prevalence of large scale unemployment in the rural sector has led one to believe that while unemployment affects both men and women alike yet female agricultural labourers are among the poorest section of the society with high unemployment rate. Unemployment also pushes a large number of women into non-institutionalised and unorganized sector to seek casual work as domestic maids, sweepers, scavengers, etc. Thus, unemployment and poverty forces a growing number of women into agriculture and to informal sector where employment competition is intense. Most of these women are employed in activities that take very specific forms where women tend to concentrate in areas of non-wage sector that suite their reproductive role and attending to extension of their domestic chores. This not only severely lower down the productivity of the women in the labour market but also their work and effort tend to remain unaccounted in the official statistics.

## OCCUPATIONAL PATTERN OF TRIBAL WOMEN IN INDIA AND MIZORAM

The tribal population of India as revealed in 2001 Census was 84 million. This constituted 8.2 per cent of the total population. Despite the protection given to the tribal population by the Constitution of India (1950), this ethnic tribal group remains one of the most backward in India based on important indicators such as health, education and income earning capabilities. The tribals are predominantly living in rural areas and the literacy rate of the tribal population is much lower than the literacy rate of the general population of the country.

The women in the tribal community constitute nearly half of the total tribal population. The well-being of the community depends importantly on the status of their women.

The data presented in Table 4.10 show the total percentage of tribal female workers which has been increasing since 1971. The same trend is found in Mizoram where the number of tribal female workers increased from 39.42 per cent in 1981 to 42.21 per cent in 1991 and again to 48.1 per cent in 2001. This implies that a larger proportion of female population who supplement their family income by working in the fields and are not counted as workers.

A comparison with other female workers reveals that share of tribal female workers is 43.18 per cent in India and 48.1 per cent in Mizoram whereas total female workers are 31.59 per cent in India and 43.7 per cent in Mizoram.

Table 4.11 shows that agriculture has remained the predominant source of livelihood among the tribal female in India. Participation of tribal women is either as cultivators or agricultural labourers, where their participation rate is almost equal in proportion to other services representing a negligible presence of less that 10 per cent. In India tribal women are mostly engaged as agricultural labourers whereas they are mostly engaged as cultivators in Mizoram.

**Table 4.10.** Tribal Female Population: A Percentage of Workers to Total Population

| Area | 1971 | 1981 | | 1991 | | 2001 | |
|---|---|---|---|---|---|---|---|
| | Main workers | Main workers | Main+Marginal workers | Main workers | Main+Marginal workers | Main workers | Main+Marginal workers |
| India | 20.75 | 28.18 | 48.33 | 29.99 | 43.71 | 23.9 | 43.18 |
| Mizoram | – | 33.8 | 39.42 | 33.00 | 42.21 | 32.3 | – |

**Table 4.11:** Tribal Female Workers: Percentage of Cultivators, Agricultural Labourers and Other Workers

| | Year | Total workers | Cultivators | Agril. Labourers | Other Workers |
|---|---|---|---|---|---|
| India | 1981 | 100 | 43.53 | 44.9 | 11.49 |
| | 1991 | 100 | 43.04 | 44.2 | 08.68 |
| | 2001 | 100 | 41.02 | 44.8 | 11.01 |
| Mizoram | 1981 | 100 | 87.49 | 0.79 | 11.72 |
| | 1991 | 100 | 83.44 | 3.29 | 13.26 |
| | 2001 | 100 | 62.01 | 6.08 | 29.03 |

*Sources:* (i) Census of India, 1971-2001, Special Tables on ST for India and NE States.

(ii) Census of India, Mizoram 1971-2001.

2001 census reveals that there has been a gradual shift towards agriculture and other related occupations in Mizoram. Shift in agriculture is indicative of the proportion of the landless workers in agriculture which again implies the percentage of seasonal and marginal workers are more among the female agricultural labourers.

In spite of a large worker percentage among tribal families, they are predominantly rural. 92.6 per cent of the tribal population are concentrated in the rural areas.[11] Though male members are still considered to be the bread winners, tribal women are economically independent. However, their independent status does not reflect in their upliftment. As compared to non-tribal females, the tribal females lack access to their resources and secured form of employment. The increased entry of women into lowest rungs of the skill hierarchy as agricultural labour and unskilled workers has only contributed to aggravating the process of marginalization that has necessitated their entry into labour force. Consequently, they have been relegated into subordinate and inferior position in terms of wage levels, employment status and intensity of work in relation to male workers. The opportunities of upward occupational mobility are virtually lacking and a lot remains to be done both in the social and economic front before the benefits of various development projects could improve the participation of the female workers in this region.

## LITERACY AND WORK PARTICIPATION RATE

Since there is a high corelationship between employment particularly in the high paid categories and educational qualifications, it is pertinent to examine the overall literacy rate of women and their influence in the labour market.

National data on literacy rate reveal that female literacy increased from 21.97 per cent in 1971 to 39.42 per cent in 1991 and further to 54.16 per cent in 2001 as against male literacy of 45.95 per cent, 63.86 per cent and 75.85

respectively for the same period. The growth of female literacy from 0.6 per cent in 1901 to almost 55 per cent in 2001 is quite significant as shown in Table 4.12. But how far has this improved female literacy contributed to improve the status of women and to remove marginalisation of female labour force needs to be analysed and examined. NSS data revealed that among illiterate, both men and women work in large number and their work participation is comparatively high. However, within immediate education group labour participation is low because a certain percentage opts for elementary education and in certain cases continues through secondary education. The participation rate of graduate is fairly high both in the rural and urban sectors. In the urban areas, the socio-economic conditions for women are more liberal but lack of availability of suitable jobs and wages often keep a large percentage of educated women out of the labour force.[12]

There has been a significant improvement in the socio-economic positions of the Mizo women, especially after the propagation of Christianity to the Mizo people by the missionaries.

The foreign missionaries adopted education as the most important means of spreading Christianity and within a short period of 50 years a significant percentage of the population of Mizoram became educated. Literacy rate of Mizoram is the second highest in the country next only to Kerala. The State of Mizoram enjoys a fairly comfortable position with respect to female literacy at 86.13 per cent that is higher than the national figure of 54.16 per cent and male literacy at 90.69 per cent as against the all-India figure of 75.85 per cent.

Through education, the socio-economic life of the people have changed for the better and besides the teaching of Christianity has slowly but steadily driven away the traditional way of life. As a result, women are now no longer completely debarred from inheriting family property.

The issue now solely depends on the decision of the parents jointly or the father or the mother of the family after the expiry of the father or mother.

Investment in education is one of the significant components in improving the quality of life. It enhances a woman's sense of her own needs and perspectives, and her power to make any family planning decisions. Besides, female education has been found to have a more significant effect on poverty reduction and promotion of sustainable development by influencing the family size and female labour force participation.

High literacy rate among the Mizo women enable them to make choices in areas like education, employment and health and enhancing access to legal literacy and equal participation in the developmental process. However, like the rest of India the percentage of female dropouts in the elementary and secondary education is rather high in the state, probably due to lack of sufficient resource and motivation to promote investment in girls' education. Moreover, in our social set up male enjoys superior social status and are considered to be a potential income earner. This set up a chain effect, adversely influencing the female status and opportunities for employment and training in general.

The distribution of female workers among different occupational activity reveals that in spite of growth of literacy, almost 65.6 per cent (2001) of female workers are engaged as cultivators. This reflects that in spite of high female literacy rate, a large percentage of the female workforce is engaged in agriculture to earn a living and thereby contribute to family income. Women's capability has been expanded over the years but this expansion is not being harnessed effectively in service more so in jobs requiring professionals, technical, administrative and managerial skill.

**Table 4.12 : Literacy Trends: 1971–2001** *(As percentages to total population)*

| | 1971 | | | 1981 | | | 1991 | | | 2001 | | |
|---|---|---|---|---|---|---|---|---|---|---|---|---|
| | T | M | F | T | M | F | T | M | F | T | M | F |
| India | 34.45 | 45.95 | 21.97 | 43.56 | 56.37 | 29.75 | 52.11 | 63.86 | 39.42 | 65.38 | 75.9 | 54.16 |
| Mizoram | 53.79 | 60.49 | 46.71 | 59.88 | 64.46 | 54.91 | 82.27 | 85.65 | 78.60 | 88.49 | 90.7 | 86.13 |
| Aizawl | — | — | — | 65.09 | 68.91 | 61.00 | 88.06 | 90.40 | 85.51 | 96.5 | 96.7 | 96.3 |
| Lunglei | — | — | — | 56.89 | 62.55 | 50.46 | 77.73 | 82.37 | 72.58 | 84.2 | 87.4 | 80.6 |
| Saiha | — | — | — | 46.09 | 37.45 | 24.58 | 59.11 | 66.14 | 51.24 | 82.2 | 86.1 | 78.1 |

*Sources* : (i) Census of India, 1971–2001.
(ii) Census of Mizoram 1971–2001.

Literacy rate in Aizawl district has long been high compared to the state of Mizoram and the country as a whole. The male literacy records the highest percentage of 96.7 per cent against the all India figure of 75.85 per cent and state figure of 90.69 per cent. Female literacy is 96.3 per cent that is better than all India figures of 54.16 per cent and state figure of 86.13 per cent. Among the three districts Aizawl has the highest literacy followed by Lunglei and Saiha. Aizawl district has been maintaining an impressive female literacy trend in comparison with the state as well as India. This perhaps is a reflection of the fact that people in this part of the State are more education-conscious and are better aware of the important role of education for socio-economic development.

In spite of the fact that literacy rate among females is high in Mizoram and FWPR is also high yet unemployment situation is acute in the State. Sizeable proportions of educated and capable manpower still need to be gainfully employed to earn minimum level of wages and income.

The role of female education in economic development has been recognized for closing the gender gap in educating by expanding educational opportunities for women is economically desirable for the following reasons[13]:

(a) *Higher Rate of Return:* The rate of return to women's education is found to be higher, on average, than that of men's in most developing countries. As yet there is no diminishing return to women's education.

(b) *Long Term Improvement in the Quality of Human Resources:* Improved child health and nutrition and more educated mothers help improve the quality of a nation's human resources over the next few generations. This is likely to have multiplier effects on the economy in the form of improvement in both the quality of the population and of life.

(c) *Breaking the Vicious Circle of Poverty:* The incidence of rural poverty in developing countries is very high among the women mainly due to landlessness. So any marked improvements in their role and status via education can break the vicious circle of poverty and inadequate schooling.

An old saying tells us that when you educate man you educate only an individual but when you educate woman you educate the whole household. This is quite significant in the context of Mizoram. Attitudes towards females and their education also witness striking difference as time goes on. Literate women are better liberated and more free from the influence of superstition or superstitious belief. So it may be said that literacy has impacted Mizo women in various positive dimensions. Investment in education is one of the significant components in improving the quality of life. It enhances a women's sense of her needs and perspectives, and her power to make any family planning decisions. High literacy rate among mizo women enable them to make choices in areas like education, employment and health enhancing access to legal literacy and equal participation in the developmental process.

NOTES

1. Rural Urban details have been tabulated in Table 4.5.
2. Davis, Nancy (1996): "Unorganised Women Workers: Problems and Prospects" in *Unorganised Women Labour,* in S.N. Tripathy (Ed), India, Discovery Publishing House, New Delhi.
3. Bhalotra, S. (1998): "The Puzzle of Jobless Growth in Indian Manufacturing", *Oxford Bulletin of Economics and Statistics,* Vol. 60, No. 1.
4. Banerjee, N. (1999): "Women in Emerging Labour Market", *The Indian Journal of Labour Economics,* Vol. 42, No. 4.
5. Hirwary, Indira (1999): "Economic Reform and Women's Work", in Papola, T.S. and Sharma A.N. (ed.) *Gender and Employment in India,* Vikas Publishing House Pvt. Ltd., New Delhi.

6. Bardhan, Kalpana (1985): "Women's Work, Welfare and Status: Forces of Tradition and Change in India", *Economic and Political Weekly*, September 14th.
7. Sunderam, K. (1996): *Inter State Variations in Workforce Participation Rate of Women in India: An Analysis*, ILO.
8. Mukhopadhyay, S. (1999): "Locating Women within Informal Sector Hierarchies", in Papola T.S. and Sharma, A.N. (ed.) *Gender and Employment in India*, Vikas Publishing House Pvt. Ltd. New Delhi.
9. Sharma, Mirian (1978): *The Politics of Inequality*, Honolulu, University of Hawaii Press, Hawaii.
10. Mies, Maria (1980): "Capitalist Development and Subsistence Reproduction, Rural Women in India", *Bulletin of Concerned Asian Scholars*, Vol. XII, No. 1.
11. Singh, A.K. (1993): *Tribes and Tribal Life*, Vol. 13, Approaches to Development in Tribal Context, Swarup & Sons, New Delhi.
12. Murli Manohar, K., (1983): *Socio-Economic Status of Indian Women*, Seema Publications, 1983.
13. Lalhriatpuii (2006): *Status of Women: Focus Mizoram – Past Trends and Desirable Perspective*, Seminar Paper on Emancipation of Women, NE-ICSSR, Shillong (being published).

# 5

# FEMALE WORK PARTICIPATION RATE IN MIZORAM
## An Empirical Analysis

### INTRODUCTION

Feminist economists have always objected to the way in which women have been incorporated into the existing framework of labour theories, since they generate conclusions, which according to them are thoroughly biased against women. Labour theories, which attempt to capture the position of women in the labour market, include women in a way, which fails to grasp the realities of women's participation in the labour market. According to the feminist economists, women's work participation which is often gender biased is considered "too natural" by the sexual division of labour; prescribed by the proponents of recently developed home economics. In a male dominated patriarchal society, male pattern of labour mobility, labour market behaviour and the institutions associated with these patterns are considered the norms of studying women's participation in the labour market as well. However, the pattern of women's participation in the labour market and its determinants may be totally different from the factors prescribed by male economists in the labour market theories. In this chapter, we have, therefore, attempted to identify some of the pertinent yet neglected and totally overlooked factors, which actually determine work participation in the labour market.

FEMALE WORK PARTICIPATION IN MIZORAM

An examination of the primary data reveals that the district of Aizawl registers the highest participation of women labour force among the three districts, viz. Aizawl, Lunglei and Saiha district. An investigation into the villages of Mizoram has revealed that participation of women in work are found everywhere and women are engaged in various forms of work such as weaving, agriculture, plantation, construction, poultry farming, piggery and also meat and vegetable vendors. According to Ghosh[1] while many works are done with the assistance of or in co-operation with the male members, there are many women who work individually on their own initiative so as to supplement their family income. Unmarried women also work under family compulsion and at many times earns so as to save their earnings for their marriage expenditure. But most of these works, which they perform, are neither not recognized nor substantially rewarded in monetary terms. The vulnerability of these works acts as a source of cheap and exploited labour class.[2] In the absence of trade unions or unionization of work, workers feel insecure and uncertain about their future jobs security. Typically, the female workers on account of their low bargaining power are subjected to the terms and conditions laid by their employers. In other words the relation between the employer and the employee is typically a relation between the "power possessor and the one who is not the bearer of such a power". This is evident in the study undertaken by Kahn,[3] who argues that though this behaviour of subordination and submission is prevalent among all sexes but it is more dominant and reflective in the case of women workers. Feminists argue that while men's employment is a necessary condition for the maintenance of a family, women's entry into the paid sector is conditional. Feminist point to the fact that, it is the only women class who are usually trapped in the stratification process and they are the most vulnerable flexible resource in the labour market.

The job scenario of female workers in Mizoram is, therefore, not very different from the all India scenario. Feminisation of the informal sector has assumed a tremendous proportion. With the adoption of the market-based economy, several traditional industries have been adversely affected through competition. Decline of those activities where women labour force play a dominant role implies that they are forced to combine several economic activities in the unorganised sector, which are extremely low paid and without any job security in an attempt to supplement their family income.

The result of all these tendencies according to Banerjee[4] is that :

(1) Women's own income has remained low because they continue to concentrate in agriculture where labour productivity has grown little;

(2) As unpaid family labour, work is not empowering for nearly half of the women engaged in traditional, family based occupations;

(3) The decline of many such household occupations has meant that women's roles in these occupations have become devalued; and

(4) The search for additional work by men often ends up by their taking over women's occupations.

All these tendencies in the labour market have only contributed in increasing the segmentation in the labour market on gender lines. Mizoram too has not been totally immune to this tendency. In an attempt to examine this tendency of segmentation of labour market in depth, we have discussed below the pattern of males and females labour market participation in Mizoram.

## LABOUR MARKET SEGMENTATION ON GENDER BASIS

It is important to examine the work participation of females and to make a comparative study with the male participation rate so as to understand the extent of labour market segmentation on gender lines. The details are tabulated in Table 5.1.

Table 5.1 documents that in the entire Mizoram and the three districts under survey, FWPR is much lower than the overall MWPR. While FWPR worked out to be 43.98 per cent MWPR is estimated at 53.80 per cent. The same trend of low participation of females has been observed for all the three districts studied in Mizoram with Saiha district registering the lowest female participation rate (42.07%). This is against the 2001 Census reports indicating FWPR of 44.7 per cent for the same district. 2001 Census report also shows that FWPR is low for all the three districts of Mizoram with Aizawl showing the lowest participation of 42.02 per cent.

**Table 5.1:** Work Participation Rate

| State/District | WPR | State/District | Urban | Rural |
|---|---|---|---|---|
| Mizoram | M | 53.80 | 56.77 | 46.63 |
| | F | 43.98 | 45.89 | 39.36 |
| Aizawl District | M | 56.19 | 58.82 | 47.37 |
| | F | 44.59 | 46.31 | 38.16 |
| Lunglei District | M | 52.68 | 54.48 | 46.22 |
| | F | 43.32 | 45.67 | 41.43 |
| Saiha District | M | 50.88 | 54.94 | 46.15 |
| | F | 42.07 | 44.94 | 42.66 |

*WPR : Work Participation Rate*
*M : Male*
*F : Female*
*Source:* Field Survey 2006.

The variation of the primary data reports could be attributed to the following factors :

The census workforce includes those who cultivate land for domestic consumption and excludes "those who produce goods for self-consumption of the family members of the household like collecting wood for fuel, fodder, grass and other forest product and selling some of them". Inclusion of their services may also contribute to the differences of the two reports.

Census 2001[5] is taken as a reference period and the sample survey has been undertaken during the years 2006-2007. The data in the present study reflects the changes over the last five years.

This trend of low participation of female workers is observed in India and Mizoram; it has been observed that in the rural areas of Mizoram, both male and female workers are engaged in agriculture related activities since this sector has high potential for absorption of women. Women find an easy access for employment in this sector. In Lunglei district alone, almost 12.5 per cent are engaged in agriculture and its related activities in the unorganised sector and the largest concentration is found in the district of Saiha (18.84%).

The low participation of females in Mizoram could be partly explained due to the following factors :

> Due to lack of education and skill and the traditional societal set-up in the villages, women are usually confined to home engaged in various household activities, which are not counted as work and hence excluded from the workforce. This can be explained in terms of socio-cultural norms and prejudices, traditional values, which govern the functioning of every society. In India, such norms and patterns determine the entry and exit of women from the labour market.[6] Among the three districts, the lowest female participation rate is found in the district of Saiha. Female WPR in Saiha is low but in other two districts the scenario is quite different. This could be due to

the fact that overall job opportunities are limited in Saiha and even in the rural areas the employment situation is very grim and, therefore, whatever job opportunities that exist are in the urban areas.

The highest female as well as male participation in Aizawl is due to its logistics advantageous and being a convenient gateway for all the other districts which probably has led to an influx of people and creation of job opportunities in and around the district. Aizawl records a high female participation of 44.59 per cent and male participation of 56.19 per cent.

The growth of WPR in the Lunglei district may also be explained due to its closeness with the borders of Bangladesh. FWPR in Lunglei is 43.32 per cent as against 52.68 per cent for male. According to 2001 Census FWPR in the area is 43.02 per cent and MWPR is 56.98 per cent. The overall economy is poorer than Aizawl District and people have limited scope to find suitable employment opportunities. As mentioned earlier Saiha recorded the lowest female participation, in certain villages within the district, the women are totally unaware of their rights to demand a price for their contribution either in the family farm or business. They narrate that their engagement in family farm or cultivation is part of their household chores and are virtually unaffected by their non-recognition as a contributor to the total production process. Therefore, non-recognition and non-remuneration of these workers leave them outside the purview of being categorized as workers though they are totally a vital contributor in the participatory process. In this manner also female workers account for a low percentage as compared to their male counterparts.

In the rural areas again, the participation of males are substantially higher than the females in all the three districts and Mizoram as a whole.[7] High participation of males could be explained on the argument that the rural economy, which is virtually an agrarian economy, has the capacity to carry a larger number of disguisedly unemployed persons at low levels of productivity and this is particularly true for women.

In urban areas, the socio-cultural prejudices against female employment are found to be less strong due to higher level of awareness that develops with high literacy and modernization and this could be one of the factors for which male-female gap is higher in rural areas.

Overall it may be said that, the under-representation or the low participation of female workers as compared to the males could be explained on line with the feminist though that patriarchy have led men to organize themselves to ensure that men maintain patriarchal power not only within the private domain but also in the public sphere, i.e. the labour market also plays a dominant factor in determining the role and position of women in the society.[8]

## THE PICTURE OF FWPR THAT EMERGES IN MIZORAM

It has been established that women constitute a strong participatory force in Mizoram along with men. The highest participation of females as well as males has been recorded in the district of Aizawl followed by Lunglei and Saiha district. The growth of urbanization and absence of sufficient work in the rural sector has led to high female participation in the urban areas in Aizawl district as compared to other districts. Rural participation is highest in the district of Saiha. Overall, the participation of women workers in the entire area is low as compared to male workers in the areas but slightly higher than the overall FWPR of India. Given the right opportunities and effective recognition of their work, women of Mizoram could emerge as a more powerful and valuable productive resource.

## FWPR AND SEX RATIO

The male female composition of population influences not only the form and tempo of life in any community but also vitally affects labour supply through marriage and fecundity.[9] The study of female ratio or sex composition is, therefore, of special importance to which we turn our attention to.

The general pattern of an adverse sex ratio as obtained in India also holds in the case of Mizoram. Of course, the excess of males over females is significantly less in Mizoram and unlike many parts of the country, the deteriorating trend in sex ratio is noticed to be improving over the years. Studies have revealed that high literacy rate; particularly female literacy has a very favourable influence on sex ratio. The slightly better sex ratio of Mizoram may thus be attributed to high female literacy and favourable social institutions. One of the conclusions that one would derive is possibly the improved literacy status in the area yielding results.

Adverse sex ratio in less developed countries including India is due to low status of women in these places, and rampant practice of gender discrimination. There is, therefore, a close link between social status, sex ratio and economic status of women. The ability to earn an income through paid employment enhances the social status of a woman, which in turn leads to a favourable sex ratio.

Therefore, it is considered that higher sex ratio has a strong positive relationship with FWPR. If the sex ratio is higher, i.e. there are more women than per thousand men, there is greater scope for increasing female participation and *vice versa*. Therefore, it implies that there exists a positive relationship between FWPR and sex ratio. The positive as well as negative role of increased female labour force participation in determining demographic outcomes such as fertility, gender bias in sex ratio are discussed widely in studies undertaken by Bardhan[10] and Miller.[11]

**Table 5.2:** Sex Ratio In Mizoram and India

| Sl. No. | Areas | Sex Ratio | On the basis of | |
|---|---|---|---|---|
| | | | Urban | Rural |
| 1 | India (Census 2001) | 933 | 900 | 945 |
| 2 | Mizoram (Census 2001) | 935 | 948 | 923 |
| 3 | Aizawl District | 984 | 980 | 1000 |
| 4 | Lunglei District | 963 | 1000 | 958 |
| 5 | Saiha District | 970 | 978 | 961 |

*Source* : Field Survey 2006.

Table 5.2, documents that among the districts of Mizoram, Aizawl has the highest level of sex ratio at 984 as against the census figure of 951 in 2001. This could partially be explained due to a relatively high literacy in the district. Among the three districts Aizawl appears to be the most literate district recording significant increase from 85.51 per cent in 1991 Census to 96.3 per cent in 2001 census for females and from 90.40 per cent to 96.7 per cent for males in the same period. Female participation is also relatively high with 42.02 per cent in 2001 Census. Lunglei, with a high sex ratio of 1000 in the urban areas, has, however, shown a relatively low growth of female work participation in the urban areas. This may be mainly due to limited opportunities in Lunglei and inadequate expansion of the economy of the district. However, it may be seen that the status of women in the district is getting better as revealed by our survey and when compared with the past history of the town.

In Saiha district, the sex ratio is 970. The female work participation rate is 42.66 per cent in the rural areas and 44.94 per cent in the urban areas, which is higher than their participation in the rural areas. This could be due to the fact that as urban concentration of worker is high, women along with male members move to the urban areas in search of better opportunities.

In Aizawl, an improved sex ratio in the urban areas speaks of greater awareness and comparatively improved standards of living among the urban people, which is reflected in a positive attitude towards the girl child. Female participation has increased proportionately as well, which is the highest in Mizoram. In urban areas, explanation that is usually provided for increased participation is that participation in remunerative employment increases the returns in investments in girls that will lower the cost of upbringing the girl child. Since the status of women is relatively better in the district, such may not be the case and hence the sex ratio in the district is much better in comparison to the all India figure.

However, though the positive relationship between a favourable sex ratio and FWPR holds good in all the three districts of the State, the percentage of FWPR on the whole is unsatisfactory. Due to the absence of urban development, the absorption of all sections of labour force is extremely slow in the valley. Improvement of sex ratio in the urban areas could also be due to migration of male to towns in search of better opportunities for living. Along with participation in work there is economic independence, which indirectly raises the status of women within and outside the household. This leads to lowering of the discrimination in favour of boys and preference towards son will be adversely affected as working women will be less dependent on sons in the old age.[12]

## FWPR AND LITERACY

The aim towards being literate is being pursued in the area with the objective to better one's chances in the labour market. The avenues of education or white colour employment exist not only within the State but also outside the region. Education is, therefore, one major way or a process of out-migration of not only the male force but also the female workforce.

A look into the literacy Table 5.3 suggests that the literacy level is reasonably high in all the three districts and Mizoram as a whole. Among the districts, Aizawl records the highest literacy percentage of 96.40 per cent. The high literacy rate in the district is obviously due to a fast growth of literacy in Aizawl followed by growth of literacy in the other blocks within the district.

**Table 5.3 :** Literacy Rate

*(in Percentage)*

| Sl. No. | State/ District | Sex | Study Areas | Urban | Rural |
|---|---|---|---|---|---|
| 1 | Mizoram | M | 94.37 | 95.42 | 91.83 |
| | | F | 92.84 | 93.10 | 92.20 |
| 2 | Aizawl | M | 97.58 | 98.03 | 96.05 |
| | | F | 96.40 | 96.49 | 96.05 |
| 3 | Lunglei | M | 94.28 | 92.59 | 92.59 |
| | | F | 91.81 | 90.00 | 90.01 |
| 4 | Saiha | M | 88.16 | 89.01 | 87.17 |
| | | F | 85.36 | 84.27 | 86.66 |

*Source :* Field Survey 2006.

The district of Lunglei is marginally behind Aizawl district in female literacy at 91.81 per cent rate this shows a promising trend of female participation of 43.32 per cent. Saiha district also records a female literacy of 85.36 per cent though FWPR worked out to be slightly lower than the other districts. It, therefore, transpires that in labour market, gender discrimination is higher in Saiha in comparison to Aizawl and Lunglei districts.

Among the three districts, Saiha shows the lowest level of female literacy of 85.36 per cent along with low female participation rate at 42.07 per cent. This also reflects that absorption of women in the job market is extremely limited in spite of women achieving a minimum level of literacy level.

In rural areas, the female work participation rate generally declines with the rise in the level of education, implying that women working outside home are considered inferior and, therefore, they participate in such activities, only out of compulsion. Our study, therefore, reveals that FWPR is low and there is at least some positive relationship between literacy rate and FWPR though the same relationship does not hold well in the rural areas.

An analysis of the relationship between female literacy rate and work participation, particularly in the rural areas reveals the confirmation of the cultural theories of the labour market which focuses attention to the socialization of women into different social and cultural values as distinct from men.

According to this theory, jobs are segregated between male and female households and market places, due to tradition, which are determined by culture and ideology. Extending further the cultural theory, Mathaei argues males and females in order to sustain their notions of their own, masculinity and feminity believe in "sex-typing" of occupations. These groups of males and females, in an attempt to maintain their masculinity and feminity prevent the opposite sex from entering their occupations, fearing that the opposite sex will contaminate their work with inappropriate gender values. Such fear is accentuated by age-old traditional values. Our interviewing of the literate women who are voluntarily unemployed outside their home particularly the rural areas due to such strong values, only confirm the basic tenets of this theory.

Overall it may be said that in the entire area women's participation is improving with the growth of literacy rate in the region. Male literacy which is only marginally higher than the female literacy reflects a comparatively higher participation of male workers in Mizoram, and this general trend is also observed in all the districts. This shows that gender discrimination exists, not only in terms of literacy but also with regard to participation rate among males and females. Gender based discrimination in various employment and occupations stem often from pre-entry discrimination against women in access to education.[13]

The relationship between literacy rate and FWPR reveals that in Mizoram, particularly in the urban areas there is a positive relationship between the two. However, an interesting finding is that in the rural areas the higher literacy the rate the lower is the female work participation. On the whole the findings that emerge from our study are that higher literacy rate has raised the status of women in the area but this has not made entry in the labour market any easier. In fact limited job opportunities both in the secondary and tertiary sectors have made the competition in the labour market and forms of discrimination may not be too evident in these sectors. Therefore, though there may be horizontal segmentation in the labour market, vertical segmentation may be absent.

## FEMALE WORK PARTICIPATION RATE (FWPR) IN THE ORGANISED AND UNORGANISED SECTORS

An unorganised sector includes all unincorporated enterprises and household industries other than the organised sector units in the private sector. Unorganised sector accounts for about 60 per cent of the total net value added in the economy.[14]

Table 5.4 shows the distribution of female workers in the organised and the unorganised sector in Mizoram and the three districts. In Mizoram almost 70.75 per cent of the total female workers surveyed are in the unorganised sector and only 29.25 per cent are employed in the organised sector.

**Table 5.4** : Job Distribution of Female Workers

*(In Percentage)*

| Sl. No. | State/ District | In Organised Sector | In Unorganised Sectors | | | |
|---|---|---|---|---|---|---|
| | | | House-holds | Private | Agri-culture | Others |
| 1 | Mizoram | 29.25 | 29.55 | 16.25 | 14.69 | 10.06 |
| 2 | Aizawl | 26.71 | 36.65 | 10.56 | 14.28 | 11.80 |
| 3 | Lunglei | 34.09 | 21.59 | 23.86 | 12.05 | 07.95 |
| 4 | Saiha | 28.99 | 23.19 | 20.29 | 18.84 | 08.69 |

*Source:* Field Survey 2006.

**Table 5.5** : Educational Level of Female Workers in Organised Sector

(In *Percentage*)

| Sl. No. | State/ District | i to iv | v to viii | ix to x | xi to xii | Grad-uate | Grad-uate + |
|---|---|---|---|---|---|---|---|
| 1 | Mizoram | 6.45 | 6.45 | 12.90 | 30.11 | 33.33 | 10.75 |
| 2 | Aizawl | 6.97 | 6.97 | 11.63 | 20.93 | 44.19 | 09.30 |
| 3 | Lunglei | 03.33 | — | 13.33 | 43.33 | 26.66 | 13.35 |
| 4 | Saiha | 10.00 | 15.00 | 15.00 | 30.00 | 20.00 | 10.00 |

*Source* : Field Survey 2006.

**Table 5.6 :** Educational Level of Female Workers In Unorganised Sector

*(In Per centage)*

| Sl. No | State/ District | i to iv | v to viii | ix to x | xi to xii | Grad- uate | Grad- uate + |
|---|---|---|---|---|---|---|---|
| 1 | Mizoram | 22.22 | 30.22 | 25.33 | 15.11 | 06.67 | 0.45 |
| 2 | Aizawl | 16.95 | 30.51 | 27.97 | 15.25 | 09.32 | — |
| 3 | Lunglei | 20.69 | 25.86 | 29.31 | 18.96 | 03.45 | 01.72 |
| 4 | Saiha | 36.74 | 34.69 | 14.29 | 10.20 | 04.08 | — |

*Source :* Field Survey 2006.

Concentration of employment in Aizawl district in the unorganised sector is equally high reaching to about 73.29 per cent followed by 71.01 per cent in Saiha district and 65.9 per cent in Lunglei district.

Therefore, all the districts in the area are dominated by a high proportion of female employment in the unorganised sector, revealing a wide gap of female employment between the two sectors. An inspection from the field survey into women's participation in different categories of job has revealed that the largest concentration of workers is in the household where almost 29.55 per cent of female workers are engaged for the area as a whole. In Aizawl district 36.65 per cent of female workers are engaged in the household activities. This is also supported from the Census of 2001 study observation where the growth of dependency of workers has been increasing in the primary sector. The primary sector is the sector, which is characterized by agriculture and its allied occupation, which is seasonal with wage rates fluctuation. A large influx on this sector signifies that a considerable proportion of female population is engaged in low paid jobs and are most often under-employed leading them to survival under acute financial crisis.

In the absence of sufficient employment opportunities a sizeable proportion of population has taken up even household jobs. As mentioned earlier, 29.55 per cent of women are engaged in household activities in Mizoram. Employment in household work also involves engagement of productive hours, which are utilized from child rearing, cooking and washing which, if translated in money terms, could have fetched a sizeable amount to the family's income. But such works are categorised as non-wage works. Studies reveal that women of all classes spend approximately half of their total working hours in household work. This also allows them to stay at relatively closer to base (i.e. home) than men. Therefore, mobility of women is also restricted in the process. A look into the nature of work that women perform at home base are usually attending poultry birds, caring and feeding herds of cattle, tending to home grown vegetables plots, collecting fuels etc. All of these activities in a way contribute to supplement the family's income. Since these sales are confined to neighbourhood or local markets these activities yield poor returns and are not accounted in official statistics.[15] Even in agriculture and household work there exists tendencies to relegate women to certain specific tasks. The social rating of these tasks and its value is determined not by the end product but whether the task has been performed by men or by women. However, women's heavy involvement in household work should not give the impression that women do not contribute significantly to productive agriculture and non-agricultural tasks.[16]

The considerably large percentage of women workers in the unorganised sector also reflects the desperation of the women workers to work being less trained and less informed. Tables 5.5 and 5.6 reveal the wide discrepancy in educational standards in the organised and unorganised sectors. Low literacy level in the unorganised sector is reflected in their participation of work which commands fewer prices in the labour market. Comparatively the educational standards set in the organised sector are better though this has not transpired into equally remunerating jobs for women. Their involvement in the unorganised sector reveals their desperation to accept the dreg of the job market. Yet it is a tyranny that all their contributions are neither recognized nor valued in monetary terms.

The economy of Mizoram, which is agriculture-dominated, reveals the experience of gender discrimination in the unorganised labour market, similar to other developing nations or regions. Though the area has been untouched by modernization of agriculture to a large extent, yet numerous changes have occurred in the rural sector of the economy of Mizoram. This has affected the work of the rural men and women belonging to the lower income group. As mentioned earlier many women, particularly during the nineties were displaced from their traditional activities. This occurred not because of technological upgradation and change in agrarian structure but due to the introduction of market economy. This has increased the workload of women in the agricultural sector.

The experience of Mizoram, like that of the other parts of the country, reveals that modernization has replaced many traditional income-earning opportunities and rural development policies and programmes do not recognize women as producers. Apart from that labour mobility and the changing patterns of work and employment are also detrimental to women workers pushing them more and more to the unorganised sectors. This is supplemented by the falling level of income of poor households, compelling the women members to take up jobs in the unorganised sectors in an attempt at increasing the income of the family. In their struggle for survival and with limited mobility, family responsibilities, social and cultural restrictions, women are compelled to take up jobs which are unremunerative and without any job security. Such tendencies in the labour markets only strengthen the operation of labour market segmentation on gender lines in Mizoram.

Organised sector is one where wages and working conditions are relatively better and job security is ensured. This sector covers enterprises, which are governed by some legislation. Around 40 per cent of factor incomes are generated in the organised sector.[17]

Total jobs, when classified over organised and unorganised sectors reveal that organised sector job represents a meagre 29.25 per cent compared with a major chunk of the working population, i.e.70.75 per cent concentrated in the unorganised sector for the entire area of Mizoram. The reason for this low concentration of females in the organised sector is perhaps due to the complex matrix of social, economic and cultural factors. The organised sector with its more lucrative and secured structure is regarded as prerogative of men's domain. As Bardhan[18] rightly points out "the ideology of patriarchy makes the exclusion from higher wages, regular jobs and trade unions acceptable to the rising numbers of women grinding away at the lowest wages, nursing only the potential access for husband or son into the privileged workforce of the organised sector". District-wise distribution of the female workers shows that the largest concentration of workers in this sector is found in the district of Lunglei (34.09 per cent) followed by Saiha district (28.99 per cent) and Aizawl district (26.71 per cent). Share of women workers in the organised sector in the district of Aizawl is comparatively low which can be attributed to:

1. Better job availability in the unorganised sector in this district compared to the other two districts.
2. Migration of female workers from the other districts to Aizawl in search of jobs due to supposedly better

economic prospects of the district. Jobs being limited in the organised sector, most of these women workers are compelled to take up petty jobs at a very low wage rate in the unorganised sector.

While sex ratio is a favourable factor in this region it is not favourably distributed in this part of the country. Mizoram with a sex ratio of 935 (2001 Census) has only 240 (2003) women workers in the organised sector. Sex ratio, which is high in the state of Kerala also, has the highest proportion of women to total employees though the State is yet to achieve gender parity in terms of employment.

In the absence of sufficient growth and development of organised sector and in the absence of keeping pace with the rapid growth of population, the organised sector has become a difficult entry point not only for women workers but also for men. In Mizoram in the absence of job opportunities, and heavy pressure of population women are left out of the organised network and are forced to eke out a marginal existence in the unorganised sector.

## DECISION MAKING AS A FACTOR DETERMINING FEMALE WORK PARTICIPATION RATE (FWPR)

Any form of national social policy which has an impact on women's work, income and welfare cannot be implemented without at the same time enlarging women's participation in decision-making. Apart from social, traditional and cultural norms that dictate the individuality of a woman there are several semi-legal and quasi-legal practices that tend to erode the decision-making power and the legal position of the women within the family. Such submissive nature predominant among women flows from concept such as male guardianship. They affect women's autonomy and authority in simple matters such as opening bank accounts for minor children, admission to schools and other civil activities of daily life. Although women are absolutely essential to the present operation of the world economy their inputs are all too frequently taken for granted and their outputs but faintly recorded.

Therefore, the ability to take decisions with regard to family affairs is vital for smooth functioning of not only an individual household but also the society as a whole and may, therefore, have a favourable impact on their WPR.

Women who have greater autonomy of taking decisions may also decide whether they should go outside the confines of their household activities and work along with their male counterparts. They also have greater autonomy in deciding the nature and type of work that they should undertake. Since the power and ability to take decision is associated with enhanced status of women, it also implies that such women may have a say when they are discriminated in their workplace.

In order to judge the capability of women in decision-making process we have taken mainly three heads, viz. the decision to spend money, decision for the purchase of household goods and decisions regarding family affairs and children. Responses to these queries help us to assess the financial independence, power and authority assigned to women within the household. Though there are other wide range of variables influencing a woman's decision-making ability, but due to limitations of time and sample size, we have restricted our analysis to three variables for the purpose of the study. A study of these factors is essential to assess the financial independence and trust conferred to women. Participation in economic activities brings in the much needed remunerative returns to the household. Though women contribute financially and productively as well to the family's output their contribution is seldom recognized or valued. "Although women are absolutely essential to the present operation of the world economy their inputs are all too frequently taken for granted and their outputs but faintly recorded."[19]

The details of decision-making as recorded during our investigation are given in Table 5.7.

**Table 5.7** : Decision-making Level of Female in Different Household Activities

(*In Percentage*)

| Sl. No. | State and District | Urban/ Rural | Spending money | Purchase of household items | Family and Children affairs |
|---|---|---|---|---|---|
| 1 | Mizoram | Total | 92.18 | 92.18 | 95.47 |
| | | Urban | 94.35 | 94.91 | 96.05 |
| | | Rural | 86.36 | 84.85 | 93.94 |
| 2 | Aizawl District | Total | 93.57 | 94.49 | 96.33 |
| | | Urban | 96.47 | 98.82 | 98.82 |
| | | Rural | 83.33 | 79.17 | 87.50 |
| 3 | Lunglei District | Total | 90.48 | 89.28 | 94.04 |
| | | Urban | 91.94 | 90.32 | 91.94 |
| | | Rural | 86.86 | 86.86 | 99.99 |
| 4 | Saiha District | Total | 92.00 | 92.00 | 96.00 |
| | | Urban | 93.33 | 93.33 | 96.67 |
| | | Rural | 90.00 | 90.00 | 95.00 |

*Source :* Field Survey 2006.

Table 5.7 indicates that in all the urban areas of Mizoram and the districts of Aizawl, Lunglei and Saiha women enjoy a greater autonomy in decision-making than women in the rural areas, although greater freedom is envisaged in matters of household consumption than spending money. Women in urban areas of Aizawl district enjoy almost cent-per-cent liberty in matters pertaining to consumption. In both the districts of Aizawl and Saiha more than 95 per cent of the decisions regarding education of the children and family related decisions are taken up by the women. Urban FWPR is also high in all the districts of Mizoram. Increased literacy in the urban areas coupled with it, stronger desire for urban life automatically entrust women to share greater responsibility and this also entails greater decision-making process in the urban areas.

Increase in FWPR is also followed by increased decision-making in all the categories of decision-making. In Saiha too, women enjoy sufficient independence with respect to decision-making capabilities.

In spite of this, FWPR is low in all the districts of Mizoram as compared to their male counterpart and the participation situation is not at all encouraging. It may, therefore, be argued that while many women are capable of taking decisions within the household, such decisions exercising power do not always gainfully translate into gainful employment in the formal sector. Though FWPR in the urban areas as a whole is high yet most of the jobs are concentrated in the unorganised sector, which are low paid and are neither steady nor certain. Women are subjected to inferior quality of work and inferior terms of employment both in terms of remuneration and benefit. Thus, though women enjoy liberty of decision-making within household such power is forced to remain dormant in the public sphere, where women lacks access and control over resources. There exists coercive gender division of labour and devaluation of their skill and labour. This results in gender inequality, which is, therefore, an outcome of asymmetry in power where men are in a position of privilege and women of subordination.

Table 5.7 further reveals that though on an average more than 90 per cent of women in Mizoram are able to decide as regards to spending and the interest of their children but the remaining 10 per cent do not possess such autonomy. Absence of independent decision-making power follows from patriarchal ideology and subordination of women. This attitude of supremacy and authority is reflected even at professional fields where women are excluded from job involving decision-making in spite of the fact that their decision levels are given much weightage in selecting the right candidate during election.[20]

An interview with the women in Mizoram, both in rural and urban has revealed that at the community level, very few of them have access to decision-making . In all the three districts surveyed, it has been observed that only women with a stable economic back up coupled with sufficient qualification, experience and age are capable of being heard at public meetings and in the rural areas aged women, and those belonging to upper strata of the society can make their presence felt or be heard. The exclusion of women from the process of decision-making at the community level speaks of a marked male bias in the ethos of the women workers in Mizoram.

### ATTITUDE OF MALE TOWARDS WOMEN'S WORK AS A FACTOR DETERMINING FWPR

Attitudes towards work are systems of meaning that are contextually derived and throw light on those contents and lead to direct them.[21] Participation in the workforce is considered to be an important factor in determining the position of an individual in the family as well as in society. It determines the level of food availability, nutrition and level of other essential demands. It holds the key to productivity .[22]

A positive attitude to women's work entrusts some degree of autonomy to a woman's status. Among lower socio-economic groups it allows for greater mobility, which enables them to compete for greater economic independence. Sociologists point out that control over income and freedom to work does not always give power and independent status since patriarchal ideologies govern the very construction of women.

It is believed that women's productivity is lower and hence, their participation will not significantly enhance the family's economic set-up. Men perceive that greater welfare is derived when women work within the confinement of their homes and fail to perceive the inner relation of income earning capabilities and welfare.

A positive attitude usually exists when women are working on their own land which is considered to be an asset generating unsatisfactory values and an instrumental orientation towards work for another.

In our survey a very satisfactory trend has been observed with respect to male's attitude towards women's work. In the overall analysis urban men depict greater positive attitude towards women's work than in the rural areas (90.5 per cent in urban areas and 87.5 per cent in rural areas). This is shown in Table 5.8. Among the three districts, Saiha depicts a higher percentage of favourable attitudes towards women's work in the urban areas (93.33 per cent) and

**Table 5.8 :** Attitude of Male Towards Female Work

(*In Percentage*)

| Sl. No. | State/District | Positive Attitude of Male Towards Female at Work | | |
|---|---|---|---|---|
| | | Total | Urban | Rural |
| 1 | Mizoram | 88.20 | 90.50 | 87.50 |
| 2 | Aizawl District | 85.32 | 91.67 | 83.70 |
| 3 | Lunglei District | 90.48 | 90.32 | 90.91 |
| 4 | Saiha District | 90.00 | 93.33 | 85.00 |

*Source :* Field Survey, 2006.

Lunglei district depicts a higher percentage of 90.91 per cent in the rural areas. Improved sex ratio in Mizoram coupled with greater literacy in the area is indicative of an improved outlook of men. With unemployment and disguised unemployment acute in the area, participation of women in outside work perhaps seems to be a necessity for the upliftment of the economic position of the households.

### AVERAGE HOUSEHOLD SIZE, MONTHLY INCOME LEVEL AND MONTHLY EXPENDITURE AND FWPR

Household size represents the number of members in the family. The larger the number of persons in the household, the greater the household's taste or need for money income and, therefore, the greater urgency can be expected for members of the family to be absorbed into participation process. The greater family responsibilities suggest that women may have a stronger propensity for market work. Like more average children per household resulting in higher responsibility for women, existence of a joint family set-up, which restricts the participation of women, more of earning male members also acts as a deterring factor for women to go into the public sphere and work. All these factors create an obstacle for women to participate. Our field findings have been tabulated as given in Table 5.9.

In our present analysis, as shown in the Table 5.9, the household size is found to be lower in urban areas of Saiha and Lunglei varying between 5.1 to 6.0, whereas in Aizawl the household size is found to be higher in the urban areas than the rural areas. The average size of the household is needed to be examined in relation to their average monthly income and expenditure pattern. With high per capita income large household size is compensated and women may not show much inclination to work or may not be forced by economic necessity to work in urban as well as rural areas. On the other hand it is also seen that large family size compels women to supplement the family income

**Table 5.9 :** Average Household Size, Income and Expenditure

| Sl. No. | State and District | Urban Rural | Average House-hold Size | Average Monthly Income (Rs.) | Average Monthly Expendi-ture (Rs.) |
|---|---|---|---|---|---|
| 1 | Mizoram | Total | 6.6 | 8558.44 | 7214.81 |
| | | Urban | 6.6 | 9515.25 | 8005.65 |
| | | Rural | 6.5 | 5992.42 | 5093.94 |
| 2 | Aizawl District | Total | 7.6 | 8635.32 | 6559.63 |
| | | Urban | 7.9 | 10596.47 | 8664.71 |
| | | Rural | 6.3 | 6062.05 | 4979.17 |
| 3 | Lunglei District | Total | 5.3 | 7732.14 | 6716.67 |
| | | Urban | 5.1 | 8540.32 | 7540.32 |
| | | Rural | 5.6 | 5454.55 | 4395.45 |
| 4 | Saiha District | Total | 6.6 | 7680.00 | 6660.00 |
| | | Urban | 6.0 | 8466.67 | 7100.00 |
| | | Rural | 7.6 | 6500.00 | 5500.00 |

*Source :* Field Survey 2006.

particularly in rural area. In our analysis, in all the districts surveyed, average urban income and expenditure are found to be higher than average rural income and expenditure. Thus it may be considered that mere household size does not contribute in the determination of female participation in work.

## INCOME AND PARTICIPATION OF WOMEN

The lower the socio-economic status of the family, the higher is the proportion of the total income contributed by women. Social customs of many communities insist that women work only if necessary for the well-being of the family. This may be the reason, which often inhibits women of higher social group or higher status to work. This may be one of the important reasons why once the rural women attain a certain level of education; their work participation rate outside their homes goes down. Attaining literacy is a higher social status according to the members belonging to lower socio-economic strata of the society. Therefore, once social status is raised it is unthinkable for women to work outside their home.

In the rural areas, in spite of possessing the requisite skills and education many women do not have the desire to work or in certain cases even not permitted to work by the patriarchal ego that dominated the traditional Indian society.[23] In the urban areas women are engaged in the formal sector, mainly when they possess the requisite skill, education and experience in such jobs. Our survey has shown that almost 33.33 per cent graduates are in the organised sector. The need for additional income provides an attraction even for women belonging to higher socio-economic groups to take up jobs in the labour market, due to increased requirements for consumer goods and for catering to the education of children as well as to keep pace with the urban standard of living.[24] Spending on all these items may, therefore, help them to raise the living standards even further.

In the rural sector, women bring cash to the family income derived from a multiplicity of secondary pursuits in the informal sector such as weaving, sewing and handloom products. Though profit margins may be small yet the proceeds contribute in a significant way for the family's subsistence living. It is thus only the compulsion of subsistence living that increases FWPR in the rural areas. Women from the villages of Saiha and Aizawl also have to travel several distances to sell their produce in the local market.

One way of identifying a measure of wealth in the rural areas is the possession of land. The possession of assets, particularly land, makes participation in labour force unattractive unless returns are commensurate with the effort. Expanded households having adequate stocks of grain may reconsider their decision of working in the fields or engaging themselves in any form of outdoor work. But those households having no such provision are obliged to work long hours or work as part-time or seasonal workers to meet minimal subsistence requirements.[25]

To cope with the increasing economic hardships women are forced to work hard and perform various types of odd jobs to eke out a living. For example, in the remote village of Saiha women and young girls supply water drawn from the river to cater to the demands of the relatively rich households for which they receive a monthly allowance of only Rs. 25, a mere pittance for such an arduous task.

Therefore, it may be argued that the decision to work will, to a large extent, depend on the relative levels of the family income. Approximately, women contribute about 25 per cent of their family income. But most of these works are dismissed as secondary work and in majority of the cases the income are spent for contingencies and other unproductive expenditures in the family. In other words, the wages raise the standard of living of the family above the basic minimum rather than ensure basic minimum itself.

The monthly per capita consumer expenditure reflects the average economic level of the State and is also a very important determinant for a woman's decision to work. As economic level of the household improves, there is a greater tendency for women to gradually withdraw from the labour force, because men prefer women to tend to their children and look after the household affairs. This also goes in line with the Neo-classical theory, which states that women's labour force participation is inversely related to one's husband's income. When the income of the family increases, women prefer more of leisure, i.e. the substitution effect is greater than the negative income effect.

In the entire Mizoram, the average monthly expenditure is high in all the urban areas spread over the three districts. Female work participation is, however, comparatively low in all the rural areas. In this connection it may be mentioned that in the urban areas, participation is mainly concentrated in the organised sector and there is a greater provision for people being engaged in secondary occupations enabling them to double their incomes. Urban life necessitates better standard of living. With higher level of income, better standard of living and provision of additional income, all these factors jointly contribute to an increase in family expenditure of a household.

In the rural areas, family expenditure is low, as also the income. With a high participation of females as well as males, female participation even if remunerated is much lower than men.

## PROBLEMS OF THE WORKING WOMEN - A FIELD REPORT

An in-depth study of the problems identified by the women under study has revealed that working conditions are not suitable for majority of the women which acts as a contributory factor for the low participation.

Women are engaged in occupations which are seasonal in nature and in the absence of scientific organization and planning they do not generate a stable income. Women do not possess assets and without financial security they have difficulty in obtaining loans and financial assistance. Similarly with the gradual introduction of machines and technical equipment on the farms, women's free entry in this sector has become difficult for them due to lack of technical knowledge in the operation of machines. Absence of child care facilities makes working in the fields and plantations more difficult and strenuous for most working mothers.

Women in Mizoram engaged in handloom productions spend considerable time in such occupations without any recognition of their skill. Women in the rural areas have limited exposure to marketing and advertising so as to command a favourable price in the market. Lack of awareness prevents these women to avail of co-operative benefits. Another serious problem affecting the productivity of the worker is that most of their works such as basket making, tailoring etc. carried on within the homes are not recognized as productive work. Consequently, the labour of women is not given due recognition nor are they protected by legislation. Moreover, most of these works are seasonal in nature; hence, casual workers predominate in the market.

Another matter of grave concern follows from the fact that with changes in the social customs, fashion as well as introduction of cheap substitute products, the survival and smooth trade of the traditional handicrafts have been threatened. While this has affected both men and women the position of women is more acute as women are the first to be displaced in the process of such changes.

The position of women who are engaged as construction workers are characterized by irregularity of employment as well as wages and they are to a large extent dependent on the mercy of the contractors and sub-contractors. The picture in the urban areas is also similar if not worse. Women working as domestic servants, sales girls, etc., have to submit themselves to the employers who fix their wages arbitrarily and with no legal protection available to them. As agricultural labourers women are often paid less than their male counterparts for the same nature of work. All these indicate that while the participation of women indicates as encouraging picture most of these works remain as casual work subjected to irregularity of payment and unstable wages. The dominance of women in these household based sectors conforms to the human capital theory with regard to the formation of human capital. Social and cultural theories could also be applied to determine the factors generating women's assigned roles in the job market.

NOTES

1. Ghosh, G.K., (1992), *Tribal and their Culture: Assam, Meghalaya and Mizoram,* Vol. 1. Ashish Publishing House, New Delhi.
2. Vanamala, M. (2000): "Informalisation and Feminization of a Formal Sector Industry : A Case Study", *EPW,* Vol. xxxvi, June 30.
3. Kahn Freund, Otto (1977): *"Labour and the Law"*, London, Stevens.
4. Banerjee, Nirmala (1995): "Women's Rights and Development Policies in India", *The Administrator,* Vol. XL, July-September.
5. *Census of India 2001,* Directorate of Census Operations, India.
6. Kundu, Amitava (1999): *Trends and Pattern of Female Employment: A Case of Organised Informalisation,* in Papola and Sharma (ed.) Vikas Publishers, New Delhi.
7. *Census of India, Mizoram 2001.*
8. Cook, J., Roberts, J. and Waylen, G. (2000): *Towards a Gendered Political Economy.*
9. Sinha, R.C. (1979): "Agricultural Development and Rural Employment", in Papola, T.S. *et al.* (ed.), *Studies on Development of U.P.,* Giri Institute of Development Studies, Lucknow.
10. Bardhan, Kalpana (1985): "Women's Work, Welfare and Status: Forces of Tradition and Change in India", *Economic and Political Weekly,* December.
11. Miller Barbara, D. (1981): *The Endangered Sex: Neglect of Female Children in Rural North India,* Cornell University Press, Ithaca.
12. Neetha, N. (1996): *Adverse Sex Ratios and Labour Market Participation of Women: Trends, Patterns and Linkages,* NLI Research Studies, V.V. Giri National Labour Institute.
13. Deshpande and Despande (1999): *Gender Based Discrimination in the Labour Market,* in Papola.

14. Economic Intelligence Service (1998); *National Income Statistics, CMIE.*

15. Jain, Devaki and Banerjee, D. (1985): *Tyranny of the Household,* Shakti Books.

16. Sen, Lina (1988): "Class and Gender in Work Time Allocation", *Economic and Political Weekly,* Vol. XXII, No. 33, August 1988.

17. Economic Intelligence Service (1998); *National Income Statistics,* CMIE.

18. Bardhan, Kalpana (1985): "Women's Work, Welfare and Status: Forces of Tradition and Change in India", *Economic and Political Weekly,* December 14.

19. Ward, Kathryn (1990): *Introduction and Overview: Women Workers and Global Restructuring,* Ithaca, ILR Press, New York.

20. Sujjaya, C. (1995): "Women's Rights and Development Policies in India", *The Administrator,* Vol. XL, July-September.

21. Denzil, Saldanha (1990): "The Socio-Economic Context of the Warli Attitude Towards Work", in Moddie, A. D. (ed.) *The Concept of Work in Indian Society,* Manohar Pulications, New Delhi.

22. Mitra, A. (1973): *The Status of Women: Literacy and Employment,* Allied Publishers, New Delhi.

23. Nelson, Julie A., (2002), "Labour, Gender and the Economic/Social Divide" in Martha Fetherolf Loutfi, *Women, Gender and Work,* ILO.

24. Hart, G.P. (1976): *Patterns of Household Labour Allocation in a Japanese Village,* Paper ADC Workshop in Household Studies, Singapore 1976, Cornell University, Ithaca.

25. *Ibid.*

6

# ANALYSIS OF FACTORS DETERMINING FEMALE WORK PARTICIPATION RATE IN MIZORAM

## INTRODUCTION

The preceding chapter has analysed the patterns and changes in Female Work Participation Rate in Mizoram comprising three districts of Aizawl, Lunglei and Saiha based on information collected from field survey. Results have been estimated using simple averages, percentages and ratios. We have used regression models which have been developed to test relative weightage of the factors determining FWPR. This allows a much more detailed test to study the effect on female work participation rates of the various socio-economic variables. The models have been examined for Mizoram as a whole and the three individual districts of Aizawl, Lunglei and Saiha.

We have introduced some variables; identify their importance and examining their effect on the work participation. Consequently, the combined effect of the variables has been examined to determine their overall effect and influence on the work participation of females.

These models attempt to examine the relationship between the work participation and female literacy, sex ratio, male literacy and two forms of individual behaviour, i.e. freedom of decision-making of females and attitude of male towards Female Work, which are assumed to affect the participation rate.

Let us first introduce the model represented by the equation :

**Model:** $W_F = a + b_1 Lit_F$.................................... (1)

Where, $W_F$ : Work Participation Rate
$Lit_F$ : Female Literacy Rate

Testing the model with the help of the primary data reveals that there exists a positive relationship between female literacy and work participation. Higher the level of literacy, higher is also the rate of participation. This supports the Human Capital Theory, which confirms that schooling leads to acquisition of productivity related skills, which increase productivity and, therefore, wages. In other words, Human Capital and screening theories both predict significantly higher earnings for the better educated. The degree of literacy among women is an important factor in their appreciation of their legal rights and in widening the range of possibilities for employment.[1] But the radical Marxism theorists confirm that there are significant differences in rates of return to education both for individual and between the sexes and racial groups.[2]

The results based on the model 1 are indicated in the Table 6.1.

**Table 6.1 :** Model: $W_F = a + b_1 Lit_F$

| Sl. No. | State/District | $a_1$ | $b_1$ | $F^e$ | $R^2$ |
|---|---|---|---|---|---|
| 1 | Mizoram | –14.68 (14.90) | 0.613 (0.163) | 14.18 | 0.47 |
| 2 | Aizawl | –250.01 (78.58) | 3.014 (0.81) | 13.84 | 0.776 |
| 3 | Lunglei | –135.28 (74.69) | 1.97 (0.84) | 5.56 | 0.58 |
| 4 | Saiha | –81.82 (43.28) | 1.46 (0.52) | 8.05 | 0.67 |

*Note :* Figures in the parentheses indicate the Standard Errors.

(i) $F_{1, 16}(0.05) = 4.49$

(ii) $F_{1,4}(0.05) = 7.71$

*Source:* Field Survey, 2006.

If estimated *F* (*F*$^e$) is greater than the tabled *F*, we reject the null hypothesis, that is, we accept that the difference between the means is significant. From this evidence we may infer that the populations, from which the samples sizes are drawn, do differ. On the other hand, if the estimated *F* (*F*$^e$) is less than the tabled *F* we accept the null hypothesis, which is we accept that the sample mean are not significantly different. In the event we may say that the sample data provide evidence that there is no significant difference between the means of the populations from which the samples are drawn.

Therefore, model 1 is acceptable both on theoretical and statistical accounts. If degree of freedom is $v_1 = 1$ and $v_2 = 4$, in Aizawl district estimated *F* (*F*$^e$) is 13.84, whereas tabled *F* is 7.71. The estimated *F* (*F*$^e$) is greater than the tabled *F* in Aizawl, therefore, we accept that the sample means is significant. In Lunglei district estimated *F* (*F*$^e$) is 5.56, whereas tabled *F* is 7.71. The estimated *F* ($F^e$) is less than the tabled *F* in Lunglei, therefore, we accept that the sample mean are not significantly different. In Saiha district estimated *F* ($F^e$) is 8.05, whereas tabled *F* is 7.71. The estimated *F* ($F^e$) is greater than the tabled *F*, therefore, we accept that the sample means is significant.

The coefficient of determination between WPR and female literacy rate is 47 per cent for Mizoram and ranges from 58 per cent to 77 per cent for the other three districts as revealed by $R^2$. The regression coefficients are statistically significant and have the required signs. The higher the literacy rate, higher is the FWPR in Aizawl and Saiha districts as well as for Mizoram as a whole.

The correlation between $Lit_F$ and FWPR emerges to be highest in case of Aizawl district which is 77.6 per cent. This relationship is further supported by primary data analysis where Aizawl records the highest percentage of female literacy (96.4 per cent). This is possible due to high growth of literacy in the town and the various villages in the districts. With the increase in literacy, women in this area are more aware to pursue a better opportunity in the labour market. Though this reflects a positive trend, yet a larger share of women participation remains in the unorganised sector of the labour market. Therefore, the increase in participation is mostly concentrated in the rural sector, which presents a rather gloomy picture of gender discrimination and inequalities. However, taking an overall picture of the area and its constituent units, it is revealed that all the three districts show almost similar pattern of relationship between female literacy and their participation rates.

The statistical validity of the model prompts us to conclude that the growth of literacy among females has a strong influence in determining their effective participation in the wage market. With regard to education, women certainly are at a disadvantageous position than men. The low rate of female literacy in India is due to the low rates of females' involvement in education and high incidence of retention.[3] It thus emerges that education can be an important factor in promoting individual participation and it may be mentioned further that along with literacy, awareness, aspiration and desire to earn also develop, creating a window to the outside world.

Thus, one may hope that Mizoram with its promising trend of literacy growth among the females, investment in women capital could bring valuable returns to the State economy. Though the difference in the structure of employment among males and females is largely determined by factors that women tend to invest more in human capital that has high non-market return and women are less likely to invest in specific human capital, so as to enhance easy entry in the labour market. This partly explains the reason why participation though increasing among females, is mostly concentrated in the low rung nature of jobs which require less skill and training.

Sex ratio or the number of females per thousand males is an important factor to determine the growth of female population over the years. Various academic discussions have given credence to the fact that in cultures where woman was allowed to work outside home either in own farm or as paid labour, the female neglect and discard was relatively low.[4] As a result the next model tested is as follows:

**Model:** $\mathbf{W_F = a + b_2 S_R}$............................(2)

Where, $W_F$ : Work Participation Rate

$S_R$ : Sex Ratio

**Table 6.2** : Model: $W_F = a + b_2S_R$

| Sl. No. | State/ District | a | b2 | $F^e$ | $R^2$ |
|---|---|---|---|---|---|
| 1 | Mizoram | –157.31 (54.27) | 0.205 (0.056) | 13.41 | 0.46 |
| 2 | Aizawl | –504.67 (208.25) | 0.562 (0.214) | 6.901 | 0.63 |
| 3 | Lunglei | –94.3 (38.17) | 0.14 (0.04) | 12.56 | 0.76 |
| 4 | Saiha | –216.46 (96.18) | 0.27 (0.1) | 7.17 | 0.64 |

*Note* : Figures in the parentheses indicate the Standard Errors.

(i) $F_{1,16}(0.05) = 4.49$

(ii) $F_{1,4}(0.05) = 7.71$

*Source:* Field Survey, 2006.

Sex ratio determines $W_F$ in Mizoram and the results as indicated in Table 6.2 reveals that the model is acceptable on statistical grounds.

If degree of freedom is $v_1 = 1$ and $v_2 = 4$, in Aizawl district estimated $F$ ($F^e$) is 6.901, whereas tabled $F$ is 7.71. The estimated $F$ ($F^e$) is less than the tabled $F$ in Aizawl, therefore, we accept that the sample means are not significant. In Lunglei district estimated $F$ ($F^e$) is 12.56, whereas tabled $F$ is 7.71. The estimated $F$ ($F^e$) is greater than the tabled $F$ therefore, we accept that the sample mean are significant in Lunglei. In Saiha district estimated $F$ ($F^e$) is 7.71 and tabled F is also 7.71. Therefore, we cannot make decisive conclusion in the case of Saiha district that there is significance difference between the sample mean.

In Aizawl district though $F$ is 6.901, $R^2$ is 63 per cent, i.e. to a great extent variability of $W_F$ is also determined by sex ratio. The sign of the coefficient is also negative in case of Aizawl district. This could be indicative of the fact that in absence of sufficier.t growth of employment opportunities in the district, a higher growth of female population lowers the chances of additional females being employed; hence participation rate does not increase proportionately. In Lunglei and Saiha district, the lack of diversification of the economy of the district and over concentration of female population in agriculture are the two basic reasons which could explain a positive correlation between sex ratio and FWPR.

The model, therefore, does support the hypothesis that an increase in sex ratio plays a positive factor in the determination of work participation among females.

Combining the two independent variables $Lit_F$ and $S_R$ we have tried to examine whether these two variables taken jointly increase the explanatory power of the independent variables. The next model tested is as follows:

**Model: $W_F = a + b_1 Lit_F + b_2 S_R$..........................(3)**

**Table 6.3.** Model : $W_F = a + b_1 Lit_F + b_2 S_R$

| Sl No | State /District | a | $b_1$ | $b_2$ | $F^e$ | $R^2$ |
|---|---|---|---|---|---|---|
| 1 | Mizoram | –152.89 (57.08) | 0.056 (0.152) | 0.196 (0.064) | 6.41 | 0.46 |
| 2 | Aizawl | –533.91 (148.188) | 1.448 (0.650) | 0.45 (0.16) | 9.345 | 0.86 |
| 3 | Lunglei | –181.7 (20.17) | 1.31 (0.24) | 0.11 (0.15) | 65.4 | 0.99 |
| 4 | Saiha | –211.35 65.45) | 0.997 (0.42) | 0.18 (0.08) | 10.56 | 0.88 |

*Note :* Figures in the parentheses indicate the Standard Errors.

(i) $F_{2,15}(0.05) = 3.68$

(ii) $F_{2,3}(0.05) = 9.55$

*Source:* Field Survey 2006.

The results as revealed in the above table (Table 6.3) indicate that this model can also be accepted.

$R^2$ has increased in this model with respect to model 1. If degree of freedom is $v_1 = 1$ and $v_2 = 4$, in Aizawl district estimated $F$ ($F^e$) is 9.34, whereas tabled F is 9.55. The estimated $F$ ($F^e$) is less than the tabled F in Aizawl, therefore, we accept that the sample means are not significantly different but $R^2$ is quite high indicating the presence of multi co-linearity between $Lit_F$ and $S_R$ in the district. In Lunglei, district estimated F ($F^e$) is 65.4, whereas tabled $F$ is 9.55. The estimated $F$ ($F^e$) is greater than the tabled F in Lunglei, therefore, we accept that the sample means is significant. In Saiha district estimated $F$ ($F^e$) is 10.56, whereas tabled $F$ is 9.55. The estimated $F$ ($F^e$) is greater than the tabled $F$, therefore, we accept that the sample means is significant. The relationship is also highly significant in Mizoram as a whole.

Freedom to take decision in family matters automatically entrusts some degree of authority to the person who takes decision. Some sociologist point out that it is poverty or dire economic necessity, and not the social patriarchal order, which confers power and entrusts women to take decisions to work. In other words, it is poverty and economic necessity, which affords freedom to a woman to decide her entry into wage market. The ability to take independent decision appears to be more common in urban than in the rural areas. On the other hand, feminists argue that patriarchal society demands that women are expected to obey rather than discuss. Regardless of the extent to which society tolerates the making or influencing of decision by women, their overt role in community village or other unit is usually minimal. Consequently, the next model is constructed:

**Model:** $\mathbf{W_F = a + b_3 D_F}$.....................(4)

Where, $W_F$ : Work Participation Rate

$D_F$ : Freedom of decision-making of females.

**Table 6.4 :** Model: $W_F = a + b_3 D_F$

| Sl. No. | State/ District | a | $b_3$ | $F^e$ | $R^2$ |
|---|---|---|---|---|---|
| 1 | Mizoram | -14.68 (14.90) | 0.613 (0.163) | 14.18 | 0.47 |
| 2 | Aizawl | -18.51 (19.25) | 0.663 (0.21) | 10.02 | 0.72 |
| 3 | Lunglei | 29.57 (59.54) | 0.12 (0.65) | 0.036 | 0.009 |
| 4 | Saiha | 0.844 (68.28) | 0.44 (0.74) | 0.34 | 0.08 |

*Note:* Figures in the parentheses indicate the Standard Errors.

(i) $F_{1,16}(0.05) = 4.49$

(ii) $F_{1,4}(0.05) = 7.71$

*Source:* Field Survey 2006.

In this model it has been observed that in Mizoram 47 per cent of FWPR can be explained by the autonomy of taking decision by women. The coefficients relating to decision-making for Mizoram as well as Aizawl district are statistically significant, and also possess their required signs. If degree of freedom is $v_1 = 1$ and $v_2 = 4$, in Aizawl district estimated *F* ($F^e$) is 10.02, whereas tabled *F* is 7.71. The estimated *F* ($F^e$) is greater than the tabled *F* in Aizawl, therefore, we accept that the sample means is significant. The position seems to be the best in Aizawl where decision-making of females has influenced 72 per cent of the FWPR. But the relationship of the model is not acceptable in Lunglei where $F^e$ is 0.036 and tabled *F* is 7.71. In Saiha estimated *F* ($F^e$) is 0.34, whereas tabled *F* is 7.71. Therefore, the sample means are not significantly different in the district. Perhaps the higher literacy rate influences the decision-making power of the females, thereby supporting the capabilities approach, which argues that with increased urbanization and literacy, women become aware of their basic capabilities, which are otherwise usually denied to them.

However, the satisfactory values of a single district do not signal a promising aspect of development.

The function is, therefore, acceptable for Mizoram and Aizawl district.

Since female literacy and freedom of decision-making have a significant impact on FWPR, and since both the functions are acceptable, the two variables $Lit_F$ and $D_F$ are included in the next model, as :

**Model:** $W_F = a + b_1 Lit_F + b_3 D_F$............................(5)

**Table 6.5 :** Model: $W_F = a + b_1 Lit_F + b_3 D_F$

| Sl. No. | State/ District | a | $b_1$ | $b_3$ | $F^e$ | $R^2$ |
|---|---|---|---|---|---|---|
| 1 | Mizoram | –33 (17.39) | 0.22 (0.125) | 0.596 (0.153) | 9.62 | 0.56 |
| 2 | Aizawl | –157.95 (15.02) | 1.55 (0.16) | 0.57 (0.044) | 166.05 | 0.99 |
| 3 | Lunglei | –144.55 (95.63) | 1.97 (0.96) | 0.11 (0.49) | 2.144 | 0.59 |
| 4 | Saiha | –81.52 (59.31) | 1.46 (0.64) | –0.005 (0.551) | 3.02 | 0.67 |

*Note :* Figures in the parentheses indicate the Standard Errors.

(i) $F_{2,15}(0.05) = 3.29$

(ii) $F_{2,3}(0.05) = 9.55$

*Source:* Field Survey, 2006.

Examining jointly the effect of the variables, in the model we find that predictive value of the function now ranges from 56 per cent in Mizoram and 99 per cent in case of Aizawl district. This is indicated in Table 6.5. Though the value of the partial regression co-efficient has gone down, in comparison to their individual function, yet they are all statistically significant and possess the necessary signs as well. For Mizoram as a whole estimated *F* is 9.62 and tabled *F* is 3.29 and for Aizawl district estimated *F* is 166.05 and tabled *F* is 9.55, hence the model can be accepted for Mizoram and Aizawl district. In Aizawl district the combined effect of the variables literacy and decision of the females to work stand out as strong explanatory variables in determining the participation of women in the labour market. The high literacy rate could be a strong causal factor explaining this behaviour. In Lunglei and Saiha districts the sample means are not significantly different.

The attitude of males towards women's work play a significant role in deciding women's entry or exit from the labour market, particularly in a patriarchal society in Mizoram.. In most societies, men express their positive attitude towards women's work provided the façade of male dominance is maintained.

Thus, in urban societies, with increased literacy, awareness and economic necessity men have been showing a positive attitude towards women's work, and in many cases men prefer working women to non-working ones because working women not only provide improved standard of living but also project an improvement of the status or well-being of the family. However in rural areas, where patriarchal influence is stronger, men tend to relate women with typical household work or what constitutes "women's work".

Taking these entire factors into account, we constructed the next model:

**Model:** $\mathbf{W_F = a + b_4 M_A}$..........................(6)

Where, $W_F$ : Work Participation Rate

$M_A$ : Male attitude towards female work participation.

The results of the model reveals (Table 6.6) that since the explanatory power of the variable now ranges from 36 per cent in case of Mizoram, 99 per cent in Aizawl district and 76 per cent in Lunglei district and the regression coefficient too has got necessary signs and is also statistically significant. The function is acceptable on all accounts and therefore, we may conclude that male attitude plays a typical behavioural attitude of a patriarchal society.

**Table 6.6 : Model: $W_F = a + b_4 M_A$**

| Sl. No. | State/District | a | $b_4$ | $F^e$ | $R^2$ |
|---|---|---|---|---|---|
| 1 | Mizoram | –13.92 (18.28) | 0.618 (0.204) | 9.17 | 0.36 |
| 2 | Aizawl | –51.73 (2.84) | 1.072 (0.032) | 1099.38 | 0.996 |
| 3 | Lunglei | –94.3 (38.17) | 0.14 (0.04) | 12.56 | 0.76 |
| 4 | Saiha | 29.446 (34.57) | 0.13 (0.38) | 0.11 | 0.03 |

*Note* : Figures in the parentheses indicate the Standard Errors.

(i) $F_{1,16}(0.05) = 4.49$

(ii) $F_{1,4}(0.05) = 7.71$

*Source:* Field Survey, 2006.

The attitude of males towards women's work is favourable in almost 100 per cent of the household surveyed in Aizawl district. From the analysis of our primary data it has been observed that the largest percentage of female workers in the organised sector concentrated in the urban sector. It may also to be noted that the coverage of the two towns, namely Aizawl and Lunglei has also contributed to the wider existence of the women workers in the organised sector. This implies that majority of the women are literate and hence their male counterparts are also assumed to be educated. Thus the positive attitude of men being positive is reflective of their understanding and assigning significance to women's work participation. In Saiha district male attitude influencing women's participation is low as compared to the other two districts and also the lowest in terms of the area's average. One factor could be due to low literacy levels of males, which is lower than the other districts. The next regression model tested is as follows:

**Model:** $W_F = a + b_1 Lit_F + b_3 D_F + b_4 M_A$..................(7)

In this model we have introduced the three independent variables $Lit_F$, $D_F$ and $M_A$ jointly into the function to examine their total impact on FWPR.

**Table 6.7 : Model: $W_F = a + b_1 Lit_F + b_3 D_F + b_4 M_A$**

| Sl No. | State/ District | a | $b_1$ | $b_3$ | $b_4$ | $F^e$ | $R^2$ |
|---|---|---|---|---|---|---|---|
| 1 | Mizoram | –48.97 (19.596) | 0.263 (0.123) | 0.372 (0.2060 | 0.366 (0.237) | 7.796 | 0.63 |
| 2 | Aizawl | –68.94 (17.63) | 0.235 (0.256) | 0.0103 (0.11) | 0.001 (0.19) | 1098.32 | 0.999 |
| 3 | Lunglei | –85.13 (58.08) | 3.09 (0.68) | 0.38 (0.29) | –2.03 (0.74) | 6.99 | 0.91 |
| 4 | Saiha | –79.39 (71.97) | 1.5 (0.78) | –0.17 (0.94) | 0.11 (0.44) | 1.4 | 0.68 |

*Note :* Figures in the parentheses indicate the Standard Errors.

(i) $F_{3,14}(0.05) = 3.29$

(ii) $F_{3,2}(0.05) = 19.2$

*Source:* Field Survey, 2006.

The results are shown in Table 6.7. The predictive value of the function has increased, as is evident from the increase in the value of $R^2$ in all the cases of Mizoram as well as the three districts. The explanatory power now ranges from 99 per cent in case of Aizawl, 91 per cent for Lunglei, 68 per cent for Saiha and 63 per cent for Mizoram as a whole. Though the value of the coefficients of $Lit_F$, $D_F$ and $M_A$ is reduced, their statistical significance is maintained. The model, therefore, is significant for Mizoram as a whole and Aizawl district and is not for Lunglei and Saiha districts. However, as mentioned above, $R^2$ is high for the two districts indicating the presence of multi co-linearity. Though multi co-linearity is not unusual in case of such economic variables yet the seriousness of the problem in this model induce us to reject this function for the districts of Saiha and Lunglei.

As female literacy has a direct influence on the participation of women in the labour market, male literacy has also assumed to create a positive impact on the participation of women workers. In many societies it has been observed that women cannot gain entry into the labour market due to various cultural and social belief practiced by various social units which are controlled and dictated by patriarchal ideology. Such ideology categorizes women's monetary work as unethical, immoral or demeaning. Whereas with education and awareness in literacy, men's view towards the concept of division of labour changes towards a more liberated outlook and are able to recognize the unfairness of male power.

In a typically patriarchal society, male literacy rate moulds the male attitude and this in turn may affect FWPR. We have, therefore, tried the next model incorporating the literacy of males as an independent variable as follows:

**Model:** $\mathbf{W_F = a + b_5 Lit_M}$..............................(8)

Where, $W_F$ : Work Participation Rate.

$Lit_M$ : The male literacy.

The estimated results (Table 6.8)reveal that the explanatory power of the variable goes down as $R^2$ is now only 0.156 for Mizoram and extremely low for Saiha district as well. The function, therefore, is unacceptable for Mizoram as a whole and for the individual district of Saiha, indicating that male literacy plays an insignificant role in determining FWPR. But the function is significant in Aizawl and Lunglei districts, where $R^2$ is as high as 78 per cent and 71 per cent in Aizawl and Lunglei respectively. This shows that male literacy do have a strong influence on FWPR in the two districts. Perhaps males in these two districts are liberal in their views and open to the ideas of female involvement in work outside the household.

**Table 6.8 :** Model: $W_F = a + b_5Lit_M$

| Sl. No. | State/ District | a | $b_5$ | $F^e$ | $R^2$ |
|---|---|---|---|---|---|
| 1 | Mizoram | 9.52 (18.54) | 0.346 (0.201) | 2.963 | 0.156 |
| 2 | Aizawl | –250.01 (78.58) | 3.014 (0.81) | 13.84 | 0.776 |
| 3 | Lunglei | –129.72 (55.19) | 1.86 (0.6) | 9.56 | 0.71 |
| 4 | Saiha | –92.21 (61.48) | 1.5 (0.77) | 4.69 | 0.54 |

*Note :* Figures in the parentheses indicate the Standard Errors.

(i) $F_{1,16}(0.05) = 4.49$

(ii) $F_{1,4}(0.05) = 7.71$

*Source:* Field Survey, 2006.

However, to test whether introduction of this independent variable of $Lit_M$ along with other independent variables discussed above, increases the explanatory power of the function, the final model is presented as follows:

**Model:** $W_F = a + b_1Lit_F + b_3D_F + b_4 M_A + b_5Lit_M$.........(9)

In comparison to model 7, where we had introduced $Lit_F$, $D_F$ and $M_A$ jointly; we have now introduced $Lit_M$ as another additional variable to assess the explanatory power of the function. The results are provided in Table 6.9.

**Table 6.9** : Model: $W_F = a + b_1Lit_F + b_3D_F + b_4 M_A + b_5Lit_M$

| Sl. No. | State/District | a | $b_1$ | $b_3$ | $b_4$ | $b_5$ | $F^e$ | $R^2$ |
|---|---|---|---|---|---|---|---|---|
| 1 | Mizoram | –50.38 (22.99) | 0.159 (0.801) | 0.364 (0.222) | 0.363 (0.247) | 0.126 (0.965) | 5.44 | 0.626 |
| 2 | Aizawl | –103.39 (37.56) | 0.449 (0.326) | 0.153 (0.173) | 0.702 (0.345) | 0.280 (0.27) | 852.39 | 0.99 |
| 3 | Lunglei | –73.87 (85.53) | 4.61 (4.79) | 0.38 (0.39) | –2.48 (1.7) | –1.15 (3.55) | 2.92 | 0.92 |
| 4 | Saiha | –102.42 (93.82) | 0.47 (1.89) | -0.57 (1.3) | –0.16 (0.69) | 1.95 (3.12) | 0.83 | 0.77 |

Note : Figures in the parentheses indicate the Standard Errors.

(i) $F_{4,13}(0.05) = 3.01$ (ii) $F_{4,1}(0.05) = 225$

*Source:* Field Survey, 2006.

The explanatory power of the variable has not improved in comparison to previous model. The function is significant for Mizoram as a whole and Aizawl district too. $R^2$ also improves for Mizoram and Aizawl district. In case of Lunglei district $R^2$ also improves to 92 per cent yet the negative sign of the coefficient compels us to reject the function. In case of Saiha district $R^2$ also improves to 77 per cent but the coefficient is insignificant, though the sign do not change. Hence, the function cannot be accepted as satisfactory model of determination of FWPR in Lunglei and Saiha districts.

The overall conclusion that may be derived is that the best fit of the function is represented by model 7 (involving female literacy, decision-making of women and attitude of males towards female work) in case of Aizawl district as well as Mizoram as a whole. In case of Lunglei and Saiha districts, however among all the models, model 3 (involving female literacy and sex ratio) seems to be the most acceptable function determining the FWPR in these districts.

## CONCLUSION

In the overall analysis it may be said that the best predictors of female labour force participation in Mizoram as a whole are female literacy, freedom to work for women, sex ratio and attitude of males towards female work. Male literacy does not hold any significant role in predicting the behaviour of women work participation.

In the case of Saiha and Lunglei districts, the best predictors of female labour force participation are female literacy and sex ratio. The attitude of males towards female work and male literacy do not play a significant role in predicting the behaviour of women participation in the labour market.

In Aizawl district, the best predictors of Female Work Participation are female literacy, decision-making of women, male attitude towards females work and male literacy. Sex ratio does not hold any significant role in predicting the behaviour of women work participation in the district.

Literacy has a strong influence on work participation and this is evident from our primary data, which shows that in all the three districts and Mizoram as a whole there exist, a high literacy rate, which is followed by high participation rate. Feminists, however, argue that even with growing literacy women's subordinate status is rooted in private property and a society smeared with sexist ideology structure.[5] Consequently, the predominant role of the patriarchal society can still be not ruled out altogether.

Our investigation relating to FWPR gives us sufficient ground to accept totally the traditional employment theories, which may be considered as gender biased. The factors, which determine the level of employment in the labour market, may explain determination of only the level of male employment. Determination of female employment requires incorporation of some more additional socio-economic factors, which have not been included so far in economic theory relating to employment and, therefore, makes the received theories incomplete and one-sided. Hence, our study attempts to fill up the long desired but often ignored gaps in Employment Theories.

It is thus observed that in our analysis male literacy does not influence significantly the determination of the participation of women workers in the labour market in Mizoram as a whole.

## NOTES

1. Dixit, Maitreya (1998): *Women and Achievement Dynamics of Participation and Partnership*, Kanishka Publishers, New Delhi.
2. King, K.E. (1972, 1990): *Labour Economics*, McMillan Press Ltd.
3. Thappar, Meenakshi (1997): Linkages between Cultures, Education and Women's Health in Urban Status, *Economic and Political Weekly*, Oct. 25, Vol. XXXII, No. 43.
4. Miller, Barabara D. (1981): *The Endangered Sex: Neglect of Female Children in Rural North India*, Ithaca, Cornell University Press.
5. Desai, Neera and Krishnaraj Maithreyi (1987): *Women and Society in India*, Ajanta, New Delhi.

# 7

# CONCLUSION

The study has shown that though women's participation has been increasing over the years their position is still lower than their male counterparts. In spite of their growing literacy, education and awareness, women are forced by societal and market norms to work under much subordinate position to their male counterparts and this trend is observed everywhere cutting across national and regional boundaries.

In the sample study of the villages of Mizoram, it has been observed that women supplement their family income by working in the fields or by carrying out the traditional work like weaving, bamboo crafts etc. But most of these works remain lowly paid, or are often unremunerated and non-recognized. Therefore, it is considered necessary to clarify the concepts of 'workers' and 'work'. The feminist economists argue that such concepts cannot merely rely on the "oars of neutrality". In an attempt to evaluate the picture of Mizoram, it has been shown that the productivity of women workers has not been harnessed in the true economic sense and the percentage of employment of women in secured and stable employment such as the organised sector is much less than men of this region. The women folk are engaged in various works along with men in both agriculture and household farming but the nature of most of these works reveal that they are small time works confined within the household and are yet to find sufficient exposure in the market. Secondary data analysis as well as primary finding dealt in Chapters 4 and 5 have explored the above facts.

The secondary data analysis has revealed that there exists significant variation in the participation of males and females. While the variation could partly be explained to differences in the concepts of 'work' used in the various censuses, female work participation is far behind that of males in the entire period of our analysis. Time series analysis of data has shown that a comparison of the growth of female work participation over the years reveals that the overall growth of FWPR has been better for the state of Mizoram as compared to India. This provides a positive socio-economic condition which implies though the general trend of FWPR is low, there is a gradual increase of women's workforce into the productive activities and hence being recognized and counted.

A comparison of the structure of occupational distribution of workers indicate that while in India, the dominance of primary sector is gradually declining, in Mizoram, this sector still employs a large section of female population. This indicates that employment in both the organised and unorganised sectors has not been able to absorb and utilize the vast potential of the productive labour force in the region. This reinforce our hypothesis of significant overcrowding of women workers towards the bottom ends of the informal sector, which is associated with low status, low wages and weak bargaining power making the position of women all the more vulnerable.

Though women exhibit a high participation along with men they are concentrated mainly in the unorganised sectors, where the economic returns are unstable. Our analysis of primary data has substantiated that gender discrimination in the labour market exists for the area. FWPR is much lower than the overall MWPR and similar trend is observed for all the districts of Aizawl, Lunglei and

Saiha. In the rural sector of Mizoram, the WPR of both the sexes like the rest of India has shown an increasing trend. Concentration of females in the rural sector implies that larger proportion of women are employed in agriculture and allied activities, which do not provide a stable form of employment. Similarly marginal workers exist for both males and females, but the figure is fairly high for women in the area, whereas proportions of marginal workers have been declining for males in India and Mizoram as well.

From the analysis of the relationship between FWPR and the factor determining it, it has been noted that literacy has positive relationship with the growth of FWPR; women's participation is not rising in proportion to increase in their literacy. The finding that emerges from the analysis of the primary data is that higher literacy rate has raised the social status of women in the State, but this has not made entry to the labour market any easier. On the other hand, in the rural areas it has been observed that with increased level of education women tend to shrink away from the labour market, to avoid the probable decline in their status of the society. This supports our hypothesis that with increased educational level of the females their work participation rates do not rise proportionately.

Results of regression models tested with the help of regression analysis reveal that the best indicators of FWPR are: (i) female literacy, (ii) freedom to work, and (iii) positive attitudes of males towards female work in the labour market.

The various facets of female participation show that the lower level of female participation in Mizoram is not only an outcome of definitional biases of work but also due to several social phenomena dominating the social structure. Such findings may also be true for other regions or countries as well.

The female work participation rate in India is much lower than the male work participation rate, and the same trend follows for the State of Mizoram and the three districts surveyed. The FWPR of Aizawl, Lunglei and Saiha districts are much behind the female work participation rate of Mizoram as a whole though the growth of female work participation has varied widely within the districts with the district of Saiha registering the maximum growth among the three districts of Mizoram according to Census reports.

Sector-wise distribution of participation rate reveals that participation is high in the unorganised sector and relatively very low in the organised sector. The occupational pattern shows that women participation as agricultural labourers has been increasing in Mizoram during 1971-2001, whereas in India their participation as agricultural labourers has been declining during the same period.

In all the districts surveyed, average urban income and expenditure are found to be higher than average rural income and expenditure. Household size does not contribute in determining female work participation both in urban and rural Mizoram. Non-working females are concentrated more in the urban areas than in the rural areas and the highest concentration of non-working females is in the district of Aizawl.

In conclusion, it may be said that female workers in Mizoram like the rest of India are reduced to marginal status in the workforce and gender participation in home-based activities and traditional production process need to be comprehensively estimated and accounted so as to ensure a better picture of women's participation rate in the area. The pattern of low female work participation as compared to male as depicted in Mizoram is consistent with the character of gender relations in different parts of the country. High literacy rate, which is a characteristic feature of the State of Kerala, also has distinguishing history of a liberated society. This has in return enhanced the social standing of women in the State and has brought about significant changes in terms of social achievements, in the form of less unequal gender relations, less patriarchal kinship systems, less male dominated property rights and greater prominence of women in influencing social, political and economic activities. The success of this State could be taken as an example to illuminate the social standing and position of the women of Mizoram, which also dominates in aspects of literacy among females and high sex ratio. These regional contrasts provide a useful means of investigation in different aspects of women's participation in the area and these experiences are but important lessons to emulate and adopt them in practice.

# BIBLIOGRAPHY


Acharya, N. (1979), *Transfer of Technology and Women Employment in India,* ICSSR Programme of Women's Studies, Mimeo.

Acharya, N.and Jose (1991), *Employment and Mobility: A Study among Workers of Low Income Households in Bombay City,* ARTEP working paper, ILO, New Delhi.

Acharya, N.(1981), 'Women Workers in the Organised and Unorganised Sectors in India', *Indian Worker,* Vol. 29. No. 23.

Acker, Joan (1988), *Class, Gender and the Relation of Distribution',* Signs 13.

Anker, Richard (2002), "Theories of Occupational Segregation by Sex", in Martha Fetherolf Loutfi (ed.), *Women, Gender and Work,* ILO, Geneva.

Bagchi (1995): *Indian Women Myth and Reality,* Sangam Books, Hyderabad.

Banerjee, N. (1985), *Women Workers in the Unorganised Sector,* Sangam Books, Hyderabad.

Banerjee, N. (1985), 'Modernisation and Marginalisation', *Social Scientist,* Vol. 13, (No. 10-11.), Oct-Nov, pp. 48 - 69.

Banerjee, N. (1995), "Women's Rights and Development Policies in India", *The Administrator,* Vol. XL, July-September.

Banerjee, N. (1995), Lauridsen (Eds*), Institution & Industrial Development: Asian Experience's,* Occasional Paper No. 16, International Development Studies, Rosskilde, University, Denmark.

Bakker, I. (1988), *Women's Employment in Comparative Perspective,* Oxford University Press, New York.

Bardhan, Kalpana (1985): 'Women's Work, Welfare and Status: Forces of Tradition and Change in India', *Economic and Political Weekly,* September 14th.

Becker, G. (1964), *The Economics of Discrimination,* University of Chicago Press, Chicago.

Becker, G. (1964), "Human Capital: A Theoretical and Empirical Analysis with Special Reference to Education", *National Bureau of Economic Research,* New York.

Benn, S.I. and Gans, G.F. (1983), *Public and Private in Social Life (ed.),* St. Martins Press, New York.

Bell, C.S. (2002), "Data on Race, Ethnicity and Gender: Caveats for the User", in M.F. Loutfi (ed.), *Women Gender and Work,* ILO, Geneva.

Bhalotra, S. (1998), "The Puzzle of Jobless Growth in Indian Manufacturing", *Oxford Bulletin of Economics and Statistics,* Vol. 60, No.1.

Cain, M.T.(1980), "The Economic Activities of Children in a Village in Bangladesh", *Rural Household Studies in Asia,* Singapore University Press.

*Census of India* (1971-2001), General Economic Tables and General Population Tables, India.

*Census of India* (1971-2001), General Economic Tables and General Population Tables, for the State of Mizoram.

Chandra, R.C. (1964), "Female Working Force of Rural Punjab", *Manpower Journal,* Vol. II, No. 4.

Commission on the Status of Women (1995), *Feminization of Unemployment*, 39th Session, New York.

Chaudhary, R.K. (1992), *Work Participation and Economic Status of Women*, Omsons Publishers, New Delhi.

Cook, J., Roberts, J. and G. Waylen (2000), *Towards a Gendered Political Economy.*

Datta Ray, B.B. (ed.) (1978), *Social and Economic Profile of N.E. India*, B.R. Publishing Corp., Delhi.

Davis, Nancy (1996), Unorganised Women Workers: Problems and Prospects in Unorganised Women Labour, in S.N. Tripathy (Ed), *India*, Discovery Publishing House, New Delhi.

Delamont, Sara (2003), *Feminist Sociology*, Sage Publication, London.

Desai, A.R (1994), *Women's Liberation and Politics of Religious Personal Laws in India*, CSSMTP, Mumbai.

Denzil, Saldanha (1990), "The Socio-Economic Context of the Warli Attitude Towards Work", in Moddie, A.D. (ed.) *The Concept of Work in Indian Society*, Manohar Publications, New Delhi.

Deshpande, S., *et al.* (1999), *Gender Based Discrimination in the Urban Labour Market in India*, in Papola and Sharma (ed), Vikas Publishing House, New Delhi.

Derek, Robinson (2002), Differences in Occupational Earnings by Sex, in Martha Fetherolf Loutfi (ed.), *Women, Gender and Work*, ILO, Geneva.

Dholakia, B.H. and Dholakia R.H. (1978), 'Inter-State Variation in Female Labour Force Participation Rates', *Indian Journal of Labour Economics*, Vol. XX, No. 4.

Dixit, Maitreya (1998), *Women and Achievement – Dynamics of Participation and Partnership*, Krishna Publishers, New Delhi.

Dreze and Sen (1996), *India Economic Development and Social Security*, Oxford University Press, New York.

Durand, J.D. and Miller, A.R. (1973), *Labour Force and Economic Development,* Population Study Centre, University of Pennsylvania (Mimeo).

Duvvury Nata (1989), "Women in Agriculture: A Review of the Indian Literature", *Economic and Political Weekly,* October.

Eapen, M. (2001), 'Women in the Informal Sector in Kerala : Need for Re-examination', *Economic and Political Weekly,* June 30.

,Economic Intelligence Service (1998*), National Income Statistics,* CMIE.

Folbre, N. (ed.) (1993), *Beyond Economic Man - Feminist Theory and Economics,* Chicago University Press, Chicago.

Folbre, M. and Nelson, J. (1993), "Introduction: the Social Construction of Economics and the Social Construction of Gender", in *Beyond Economic Feminist Theory and Economics,* Chicago University Press, Chicago.

Fong, M.S. (1975*), 'Female Labour Force Participation in a Modernizing Society: Malaya and Singapore'*, No. 34. Paper of the East West Population Institute, 1921-1957.

Frances, I. Jeanne (1994), "Working and Living for the Family, Gender, Work and Education", *Indian Journal of Gender Studies,* Vol. 1, No. 1.

Ghosh, B. and Mukhopadhyay (1982), *Sources and Variation in Female Participation Rate: A Decomposition Analysis,* paper for the Seminar on Women's Work and Employment, Indian Social Studies.

Ghosh, B. and Mukhopadhya, S.K. (1984), "Displacement of the Female in the Indian Labour Force", *Economic and Political Weekly,* Vol. XIX, No. 47, November.

Ghosh, B. and Mukhopadhaya, S.(1990), "Share of Women in Income Employment and Work: A Macro-Micro Economic Inquiry", *Samya Shakti, A Journal of Women's Studies,* Vols. IV and V.

Ghosh, G.K.(1992), *Tribal and their Culture: Assam, Meghalaya and Mizoram*, Vol. 1, Ashish Publication, New Delhi.

Gopalan, Sarala (1995), *Women and Employment in India*, Har Anand Publications, New Delhi.

Gulati, Leela (1975), "Female Work Participation: A Study of Inter-State Differences", *Economic and Political Weekly*, Vol. X, Nos. 1 & 2, January.

Gunderson, M. (1989), "Male and Female Wage Differential and Policy Responses", *Journal of Economic Literature*, Vol. 24, No. 1.

Gupta, A.K. (1986), *Women and Society: The Development Perspective*, Criterion Publications, Delhi.

Gupta, R.N. (1984), "Correlates of Female Participation in Economic Activity", *Indian Labour Journal*, Vol. 25, No. 3, March.

Hart, G.P. (1976), *Patterns of Household Labour Allocation in a Japanese Village*, Paper ADC Workshop in Household Studies, Singapore, 1976, Cornell University, Ithaca.

Hartmann, Heidi (1969), *The Family as the Locus of Gender, Class and Political Struggle: The Example of Housework*, in Anne C. Herrmann and Abigail J. Stewart, Westview Press, USA.

Hirwary, Indira (1999), 'Economic Reform and Women's Work', in Papola T.S. and Sharma A.N. (ed.) *Gender and Employment in India*, Vikas Publishing House Pvt. Ltd., New Delhi.

Indian Labour Journal (1999), Globalisation has changed the Pattern of Women's Employment, Labour Bureau, Ministry of Labour, Govt. of India, January Issue.

ILO (1987), *World Labour Report*, Oxford University Press.

Iyer, K.V., (1967), "The Increasing Role of Women in Economic and Social Development", *Social Welfare*, Vol. 14, No. 7.

Jain, Devaki (1975), *From Dissociation to Rehabilitation*, Allied Publishers, New Delhi.

Jayaweera, S. (1997), *Education and Training, United Nations Commission on the Status of Women*, 41st Session, New York.

Jhabwala, R. and R.K. Subramanyam (2000), *The Unorganised Sector: Work Security and Social Protection*, Sage Publications, New Delhi.

John E. Mary (1996), "Gender and Development in India, 1970s – 1990s some reflections on the constitutive role of contents", *Economic and Political Weekly.*

Jose, A.V. (1987), *Limited Options: Women Workers in Rural India*, ILO, ARTEP, New Delhi.

Kalpagam, U. (1997), *Informal Sector: Emerging Perspective in Development*, Seminar Paper, Dec. 22-24, IAMR-IHD, New Delhi.

Kahn, F. Otto (1977), *Labour and the Law*, London, Stevens.

King, E. and M. Hill (1993), *Women's Education in Developing Countries*, John Hopkins Press for the World Bank, Washington D.C.

King, J.E. (1990), *Labour Economics*, McMillan Press Ltd.

Kingdon, Geeta Gandhi(1999), 'Labour Force Participation, Returns to Education and Sex Discrimination' in *Gender and Employment in India*, T.S. Papola and A.N. Sharma (Ed.), Vikas Publishing House, New Delhi.

Krishna, A.P. (1983), "Women Technology and Development Process", *Economic and Political Weekly*, Vol. XIV.

Krishnan, S. (1990), 'Women Workers in the Manufacturing Sectors: A district level Analysis of Selected States 1981', *CSRD*, JNU, New Delhi.

Krishna Raj, M. (1980), *Approaches to Self-Reliance: Some Urban Models,* Popular Prakashan, Bombay.

Kundu, Amitab (1999), *Trends and Pattern of Female Employment: A Case of Organised Informalisation,* in Papola and Sharma (ed.) Vikas Publishers, New Delhi.

Lalhriatpuii (2006), *Status of Women: Focus Mizoram - Past Trends and Desirable Perspective,* Seminar Paper on 'Emancipation of Women' NE-ICSSR, Shillong.

Lalitha Devi, V. (1982), *Status and Employment of Women in India,* Vikas Publishers, New Delhi.

Leon, C.B. (1981), "The Employment-Population Ratio: It's Value in Labour Force Analysis", *Monthly Labour Review,* Vol. 104, No. 2.

Leftwich, H. Richard, Ansel and Sharp M. (1984), *Economic of Social Issues,* Business Publications, Plano, Texas.

Madheswaran, S. and Shroff Sangeeta (2000), "Education Employment and Earnings for Scientific and Technical Workforce in India: Gender Issues", *The Indian Journal of Labour Economics,* Vol. 43, No. 1.

Mies, Maria (1980), Capitalist Development and Subsistence Reproduction, Rural Women in India, *Bulletin of Concerned Asian Scholars,* Vol. XII, No. 1.

Miller (1981), *The Endangered Sex: Neglect of Female Children in Rural North India,* Ithaca, Cornell University Press.

Mincer, (1962), *Labour Force Participation of Married Women,* Paper in the NBER Volume, Aspects of Labour Economic, Princeton University Press, Houston.

Mincer, J. and Polacheck, S.W. (1974), "Family Investments in Human Capital, Earnings of Women", *Journal of Political Economy.*

Mitra, A., *et al.* (1979), *The Status of Women, Household and Non-household Economic Activity,* Allied Publishers, New Delhi.

Mitra, A. (1995), *Labour and Development*, Vol. 1, No. 1, July-December, V.V. Giri National Labour Institute.

Mitra, A. (1973), *The Status of Women: Literacy and Employment*, Allied Publishers, New Delhi.

Mitra, J. (1997), *Women and Society, Equality and Empowerment*, Kanishka Publishers, New Delhi.

Mitra, Pathak *et al.* (1980), *Status of Women Shifts in Occupational Pattern during 1961-1991*, ICSSR, New Delhi.

Mukhopadhya, Swapna (1997), *In the Name of Justice: Women and Law in Society*, Manohar Publishers, New Delhi.

Mukhopadhyay, S. (1999), "Locating Women within Informal Sector Hierarchies", in Papola T.S. and Sharma A.N. (ed.) *Gender and Employment in India*, Vikas Publishing House Pvt. Ltd., New Delhi.

Murli Manohar, K. (1983), Socio-Economic Status of Indian Women, Seema Publications, New Delhi.

Nath, Kamala (1968), "Women in the Working Force in India", *Economic and Political Weekly*, Vol. 3, No. 31.

Nayak, Jossie Tellis (1979), *Towards Self-Reliance–Income Generation for Women*, Indian Social Institute, New Delhi.

Nelson, Julie A. (2002), "Labour, Gender and the Economic/ Social divide", in Martha Fetherolf Loutfi, *Women, Gender and Work*, ILO.

Neetha, N. (1996), *Adverse Sex Ratios and Labour Market Participation of Women: Trends Patterns and Linkages*, NLI Research Studies,V.V. Giri National Labour Institute.

Nye, F. Ivan and Hoffman, L.M. (1972), *The Employed Mother in America*, Chicago, Rand McNally.

Orden, R. and Broadburn, N.M. (1968),"Working Wives and Marriage Happiness", *The American Journal of Sociology*, Vol. 74.

Papola, T.S. and Sharma A. (1999), *Gender and Employment in India*, Vikas Publishing House, New Delhi.

Paukert, Liba (1984), *The Employment and Unemployment of Women in OECD Countries*, OECD, France.

Phelps, E.S. (1972), "The Statistical Theory of Racism and Sexism", *American Economic Review*, Vol. 62, No. 4.

Reddy, C. Ragunatha (1973), *Changing Status of Educational Working Women*, B.R. Publishing Corporation, Delhi.

Rehman, Kanta (1995), "Gender Discrimination and Development Process", in *Labour and Development*, Vol. I, No. I, July-Dec.

Rothbeck, S. and Sarthi, A. (1999), "Gender Based Segregation in the Indian Labour Market", *Indian Journal of Labour Economics*, Vol. 42, No. 4.

Saksena, P.K. (1991), *Regional Disparities in Female Work Participation Rate in India*, Discovery Publishing House, New Delhi.

Sarkar, Lotika (1995), *Women's Movement and the Legal Process*, Occasional Paper No. 24, CWDS, New Delhi.

Schultz, T.P. (1993), *Returns to Women's Education*, Chapter 2 in King and Hill (Ed.), John Hopkins Press for World Bank, Washington D.C.

Shah, M.S. (1975), "Wages and Employment of Women in India", *Indian Labour Journal*, 16, No. 2.

Sharma, A. and Singh, S. (1993), "Women and Work: Changing Scenario in India", *Indian Society of Labour Economics*, B.R. Publications, New Delhi.

Sharma, Mirian (1978), *The Politics of Inequality*, Honolulu, University of Hawaii Press, Hawaii.

Sheikh, A.M. (1999), *Human Resource Development and Management*, S. Chand & Co., New Delhi.

Singh, A.K. (1993), *Tribes and Tribal Life*, Vol. 13, Approaches to Development in Tribal Context, Swarup and Sons, New Delhi.

Sinha, R.C. (1979), "Agricultural Development and Rural Employment", in Papola, T.S. *et al.* (ed.), *Studies on Development of U.P.*, Giri Institute of Development Studies, Lucknow.

Sinha, J.N. (1965), "Rural Employment Planning Dimensions and Constraints", *Economic and Political Weekly*, Vol. VI, No. 6, Annual Number.

Sloane, P.J. (1985), "Discrimination in the Labour Market", in D. Carline *et al.* (eds.) *Labour Economics*, Harloro, Longman.

*Statistical Handbook of Mizoram* (1971-2006), Directorate of Economics and Statistics, Govt. of Mizoram.

Sujjaya, C. (1995), "Women's Rights and Development Policies in India", *The Administrator*, Vol. XL, July-September.

Sunderam, K. (1996), *Inter-State Variations in Workforce Participation Rate of Women in India: An Analysis*, ILO.

Thappar, Meenakshi (1997), "Linkages between Cultures, Education and Women's Health in Urban Status", *Economic and Political Weekly*, Vol. XXXII, No. 43.

Thurow, Lester C. (1975), *Poverty and Discrimination*, D.C. Brooklyn Institution, Washington.

Tilak Jandhyala, B.G. (1980), "Education and Labour Market Discrimination", *Indian Journal of Industrial Relations*, Vol. XVI, 1, July 1980.

UNDP (Dhaka) (1994), *Report on Human Development in Bangladesh: Empowerment of Women*, Dhaka, UNDP.

Unni, J. (2001), "Gender and Informality in Labour Market in South Asia", *Economics and Political Weekly*, No. 26, 30th June.

Vanamala, M. (2000), "Informalisation and Feminization of a Formal Sector Industry: A Case Study", *Economics and Political Weekly*, Vol. xxxvi, June 30.

Verier, Elwin (1976), *Tribal Women in Indian Women*, edited by Jain, Devaki, Delhi: Publications Division, Ministry of Information and Broadcasting, Govt. of India, 1976 (reprint).

Viswanathan, Aparna (1992), "Sex Discrimination in Employment: No Legal Protection", *Economic and Political Weekly*, May 2.

Ward, Kathryn (1990), *Introduction and Overview: Women Workers and Global Restructuring*, Ithaca, ILR Press, New York.

Whyte, Robert and Pauline Whyte (1982), *The Women of Rural Asia*, West View Press, Boulder, Colorado.

Wollstone Craft, Mary (1975), *Vindication of the Rights of Women*, Pelican, London.

# INDEX